Praise for
Prop

Conrad Kanagy has created a wonderful biography that illumines Walter's intellectual growth with so many sources of heat and light. He has done marvelously well in opening Brueggemann's thought to readers, showing points of development, streams of influence, places of contrast and contradiction, and the ways that Walter took a bulldozer to the field for the benefit of all. The narrative moves along quickly and dramatically and shows the wondrous talents and goodness of the man.
—Kathleen M. O'Connor, William Marcellus
McPheeters Professor of Old Testament,
emerita, Columbia Theological Seminary

Conrad Kanagy has done excellent work. His emphasis on *Prophetic Imagination* throughout Brueggemann's biography is clear and compelling. His identification of key themes and questions in Brueggemann's career is insightful: especially the relationship between God's sovereignty and God's faithfulness, which he contextualizes with discussion of Brueggemann's relationship with Terry Fretheim. The inclusion of nine new prayers of Brueggemann is just icing on the cake. The narrative Kanagy has constructed sheds light on the way Brueggemann's family history impacted his life and thought.
—Samuel E. Balentine, Professor of Old Testament,
emeritus, Union Presbyterian Seminary

Here we see biblical scholarship embedded in a contemporary life of struggle, conviction, commitment, and prayer. For preachers, teachers, scholars, readers who cannot leave the Bible alone because God won't leave them alone, this book helps us make sense of our experience and our sense of what is still possible with God.
—Ellen F. Davis, Amos Ragan Kearns Distinguished Professor
of Bible and Practical Theology, Duke Divinity School

Walter Brueggemann is the clearest biblical prophet of our time. He is not just a magnificent scholar of the prophets or their best theological interpreter, but Brueggemann himself is a prophet to and for our troublesome days. Walter would be the first to deny such accolades. And this is why Conrad Kanagy's theological biography is so needed. Kanagy, in rich and critical detail, documents what Brueggemann has seen and heard, studied and learned, reflected upon and then preached and written. This book reveals what it looks like to speak the Word of God's truth to power in the face of all our ideological manifestations of falsehood. As with the prophets, justice is his measure and the marginalized are his focus. Yet, as Kanagy shows, Walter is a kind man who walks humbly with his God.

—Jim Wallis, inaugural chair and founding director of the Center on Faith and Justice at Georgetown University

I can think of no biblical scholar more worthy of a biography than Walter Brueggemann, the most gifted, insightful, and prolific scholar the field of Old Testament studies has ever seen. Conrad Kanagy has provided us with just that in a volume that is equal parts biography of Brueggemann, an account of his career, and reflection on his breakthrough book, *The Prophetic Imagination*—all written in an engaging, lively style. Kanagy's treatment consistently delivers profound insights into all three of these things (and their remarkable interrelations) and is especially noteworthy in its attention to Brueggemann's early years: how formative his family of origin, his upbringing, and his pre-professorial days were to all that followed. Even if you know Walter and his work well—or just *think* you do—be prepared to learn an immense amount in this book, which left me yet again awed and inspired by one whom I deem no less than a modern-day prophet.

—Brent A. Strawn, D. Moody Smith Distinguished Professor of Old Testament; professor of law, Duke University

WALTER BRUEGGEMANN'S
PROPHETIC IMAGINATION

Conrad L. Kanagy

Foreword
Reverend Dr. Samuel Wells

WALTER BRUEGGEMANN'S PROPHETIC IMAGINATION

A Theological Biography

FORTRESS PRESS
Minneapolis

WALTER BRUEGGEMANN'S PROPHETIC
IMAGINATION
A Theological Biography

Library of Congress Control Number: 2023933163 (print)

Cover image: Photo of Walter Brueggemann by Daniel
Sheehan, March 21, 2013
Cover design: Kristin Miller

Print ISBN: 978-1-5064-9378-7
eBook ISBN: 978-1-5064-9379-4

To Walter
On behalf of all to whom you have given the courage to
imagine God's alternative reality

Contents

Foreword

Reverend Dr. Samuel Wells
Vicar of St. Martins-of-the-Fields

Walter Brueggemann is a shy man; but he's got into a good number of fights. He's a kind man; but he's demolished the contentions of those he believes are wrong. He's quite at home in the back pew of a provincial church; but he's a preacher and prophet who's unsettled many and stirred even more. He's a radical thinker; but he's more than anything a student of the Scriptures. He's a capable leader and manager; but he's most at home reading and writing in seclusion and peace. He's a gentle grandfather; but he has the eye of a hawk and the beard of a biblical tablet-breaker.

I can't help but imitate Walter's characteristic exegetical style and revert to italicized assertions in place of subheadings. *Walter believes in God.* Among the most fascinating of this book's many diversions is its discussion of whether Walter places God's sovereignty ahead of God's faithfulness. If he does it's because he believes in the God of the Bible. *Walter believes in the God of the Scriptures.* A great many, perhaps most of the progressives who've gobbled up Walter's exegesis have stepped off the bus when it comes to wrestling with the most troublesome Old Testament texts and preferred a

blander, more anodyne God. Not Walter: his most con-
troversial statements arise from his commitment to let
the Bible speak and invite us to deal with it, rather than
sanitize and refract to render a more wholesome deity.
Walter is a theologian and not simply a biblical scholar.
What makes his work stand out is not just his offering
such a dynamic alternative to historical criticism, nor
just his ability to integrate secular analyses into exegesis, but the profoundly theological scope of his project,
which makes his books required reading for those who
study across the seminary curriculum.

Walter believes in the church. Despite his father's
experience of being patronized and poorly paid as a pastor, brought out so well in this book, Walter spent his
whole teaching life at seminaries, largely preparing candidates for ordained ministry. He never took the route
of one who may well have felt the church unworthy of
the gospel it proclaimed; he never moved institutions to
advance scholarship away from the incarnational realities of church. *Walter gladly draws on the insights of contemporary and historical secular thought*—for his quest
is to stand under the arresting and transforming word
of the Scripture, not to decide in advance what it's supposed to say and find ways to make it say so. His career
has been alive and active, sharp as a sword—and the
richer because as you picked up his hundredth book you
couldn't be sure it wouldn't offer a new set of prophecies
in tension with a number of his previous ones.

In more complex ways, *Walter retains the abiding
shame, inhibition, and ambiguity attributable to the desire
to please a mother impossible to please and a father he
wanted never to feel small.* Most people who've read his
books or attended his lectures or sat under his sermons
see Walter as a towering figure, missing only sandals
and a crooked finger to be hectoring prophet of the Old

Testament. But as this book demonstrates, Walter is very much a human being with his own family systems to experience and endure, all too aware of the difficulty of offering one's true identity to a public that only wants to see you as a warrior for its causes. Likewise, and correspondingly, *Walter inspires an affection in his friends that transcends his stellar contribution to his field.* This book describes friendships among colleagues, mentees, pastors, and those beyond the academy and church. It is as a friend that Walter is best honored, because, in the end, he is forever a friend of God.

Conrad Kanagy has done us all a deep service by asking Walter a string of questions many would love to know the answers to, by explaining many things that were previously mysterious, and by letting the person behind the public persona speak and joke and reflect. He hasn't remained in awe of his subject, but has pondered and wondered and reevaluated and speculated, the better to weigh the significant and separate it out from the transitory. This is a book to deepen our respect, enhance our understanding, and kindle our love.

Preface

Since nothing interesting has happened in my life, the
book will mainly be about my thinking and writing.
                                        Walter Brueggemann

I first met Walter Brueggemann in the library stacks
of Elizabethtown College. It was 2006, and I was
directing a sociological profile of my Mennonite denomination.[1] The results revealed only bad news across the
previous three decades. Rapidly aging members. Youth
leaving the church in droves. Racism—both overt and
covert. Little confessional life among members. Little
witness of the Gospel to the world. A loss of pacifism
and a commitment to nonviolence. And beneath it all,
a people who once embraced the separation of church
and state, now rapidly moving toward the Religious
Right.

How to explain all this bad news? What possible
framework to place it within? Where was the hope for
the church? What if God was dismantling the church
because of its mission drift, idolatry, and disregard
for the oppressed and marginalized? What was God's
word for this reality that lay in front of the church?
What would denominational leaders say about the
investment they had made if I didn't discover some
good news?

DISCOVERING BRUEGGEMANN

In response, all I could hear in my head and heart was "Jeremiah, Jeremiah, Jeremiah." So I went to the library to find the prophet Jeremiah, or at least the answer to why I kept hearing his name. I found a host of Jeremiah commentaries. But with little theological training, what sources should I consult? After hours of reading vacuous volumes about the genre of Jeremiah, debates over history and authorship and period, and the irrelevancy of the text for the contemporary world, I felt lost. Had I been hearing wrong? Should I just describe the data and turn the project back to the denomination bureaucrats to put on the shelf? Or does God want to say something to the church through this project? I pressed on.

I got to authors' last names beginning with "B." The name Brueggemann showed up. And then again. And again. And yet again. Were all of these books on Jeremiah by the same character, or was it a family of Brueggemann scholars all writing about Jeremiah? Good Lord! Here was an entire shelf by the same author and about the book and prophet Jeremiah! If for no other reason than the sheer number of books, I would be a fool not to pull something off the shelf by this guy. But with a name like Brueggemann, he was probably a German free-thinking theologian with an ax to grind about the integrity of the biblical text. But it was getting late, so I grabbed a book entitled *The Prophetic Imagination.*[2]

I began to read. And kept reading. I couldn't put the book down. The prose was readable and even enjoyable—not cursed with scholarly jargon and historical and archeological data. The author clearly took the biblical text seriously. And he was applying it to the contemporary world. I finally pulled away from the book, thinking that I may have found what I'd been looking for! I had no idea that the book had sold a million copies, was the author's breakthrough book, and had contributed to a transformation in the field of biblical studies. Nor did I know that the author was considered among the leading theologians of the twentieth century. All I knew was that the book spoke to me as a word for the church and the synagogue. And that the guy who wrote it had written a damn lot of books!

The Prophetic Imagination revealed that perhaps God was in the middle of the church mess I had uncovered.[3] Perhaps God was even responsible for the mess! If God could orchestrate the exile of God's people from their homeland in 587 BCE, who is to say God wasn't exiling the church today? What if the sins of God's people then were the dynamic equivalents for God's people today? Failure to embrace the immigrant and stranger. Rejecting the care of widows and orphans. Hunkering down in the affluence of a middle-class center and denying opportunities to those on the margins. Creating seats of power where decisions impacted people of color who had no say in the matter. Aligning with the political power of the empire while rejecting God? Men using their power to create a "legitimizing construct" and ideology that reinforced their position over women and children, creating contexts for secret abuse? Using the Bible as ammunition against the other rather than as the bread of life for all. Abandoning Jubilee because it redistributed wealth and set captives free in the way Karl Marx thought things should go? Rejecting "history-making" prophets who see an alternative reality to the one in front of them, and through their words help create that new reality. Choosing instead "history-stopping" denominational bureaucrats who deny that God's words have anything to offer anymore.[4] Laughing at the possibility that the church's exile might be God's missional moment for Babylon. Forgetting that whether shalom comes back around to God's people depends on whether they see their enemies as friends or the other. Absorbing the "royal consciousness" of earthly empires with biblical language that rejects the true "scroll power" of the text. I published my analysis in 2007, relying heavily upon Brueggemann. The book was well received, including by my own congregation where I served as pastor from 2000 to 2005.

A BONHOEFFER MOMENT?

But by the summer of 2021, I agonized as I prepared to preach a sermon on racism. What would happen if I preached what I had long taught my students about race and racism? Would I still be a pastor after the next day? During the George W. Bush years, I had cautioned the congregation about their post-9/11 political commitments to the empire. I warned that the Third Reich might not be far away from the American context. I preached against the kind of civil religion that created a syncretized Christian faith. I confronted a former pastor publicly who stood up during the "sharing time" to advocate for a Republican candidate. Addressing the empire's slow creep into the church was not new to me. But no one was critical of my messages at the time. The former pastor and I publicly reconciled and embraced. White nationalism seemed far away. I wondered if I was being apocalyptic.

But as I lay in bed that night in 2021 before preaching my sermon against racism, I knew that the atmosphere had changed dramatically in the last decade. With the election of Barak Obama as US president, voices arose spouting the old racist sentiments of what seemed like an ancient time. Conservative talk radio had propagated the "birther" lie. Racist slurs against the president become acceptable. Marginalized white supremacy rhetoric became mainstream quickly. Fox News recognized the gains in commodifying hate. And Donald Trump was beginning to stir up a white evangelicalism that saw itself losing ground to secularism and the browning of the country. White nationalism was on the rise across the American church.

Few imagined that Trump would win the 2016 election. Pastors didn't recognize how much their people had absorbed the shifting winds of the culture. Few pastors understood the risks that lay ahead for them. That a message they preached in 2005 would be heard differently in 2020. That a message received or at least tolerated a decade earlier could lead to the firing of a pastor today.

The empire had domesticated and coopted the American church through its rhetoric of fear of the other, claims of marginalization of white folks, and the promise of an alternative reality. The problem was that the alternative reality as described by President Trump at his inauguration sounded more like hell than heaven. Like Satan's reign more than like God's. But white evangelicals cheered more loudly than anyone. This was the King of Persia come to lead God's people out of the exile of a rapidly browning country. Perhaps the road to the Kingdom ran through the Armageddon-like landscape that Donald Trump imagined ahead. Even historic Anabaptists in my neck of the woods fell at Trump's feet.

So I knew I had a reason for concern. Some in our congregation had come under Trump's spell. Still, as I entered the pulpit, with the congregation meeting outside due to COVID-19, I underestimated the coming backlash. My sermon reflected upon the Jeffersonian hypothesis that African enslaved peoples were less intelligent than white people, but he was satisfied to have science decide. Race science would decide and its unanimity about the superiority of whiteness became the basis of Hitler's "Jewish solution." I shared how evangelical abolitionists of the nineteenth century had fought for an end to slavery. One of the founding brothers of Wheaton College had been beaten just up the road in Harrisburg, for preaching his abolitionist views. My text was Ephesians 2–3. The mystery of the Gospel is the dismantling of the dividing wall between powerful and powerless, crucifiers and crucified, oppressors and oppressed, men and women, Jew and Gentile, slave and free. I asked, tremoring from Parkinson's disease: "What is the mystery of the Gospel that we have missed by embracing the rhetoric of hate and division?"

Just as the sermon reached its climax, along with my anxiety, the bells of a local church began to toll "A Mighty Fortress Is Our God." As the bells rang, I could not compete. I stopped, and for a moment everyone heard "and though this world with devils filled should threaten to undo us, we will not fear . . . one little Word shall fell them." And in the silence of that moment, I remembered that the Word came not to raise an army against or for an empire. Instead, the Word sneaked quietly and unnoticed into the world. And it ambushed those powers from below by a greater power—the power of love. Not by rage, division, or discord. At that moment I glimpsed that alternative Kingdom about which Brueggemann had been writing for nearly forty years. He had drilled, drilled, and drilled the same imaginative message while hearing and sharing it anew for each generation.

When I left the pulpit I was approached by an agitated white couple who complained that they felt condemned by his message. But when I turned away I met an African friend who thanked me profusely for the message. It had comforted him. At that moment the "color line" of W. E. B. Du Bois revealed itself.[5] I had run up against it. And what arrived in my inbox that week from agitated white parishioners reminded me of just how far over I had stepped. A congregation in a small northern community that had been a "sundown town" into the 1960s was not yet ready for this message. I would later receive an agitated letter from the leader of the local ministerium condemning my message of anti-racism and white supremacy. That leader had helped to organize four buses of local evangelicals for the rally in Washington, DC, on January 6, 2021.

Interestingly, I had expressed these same views fifteen years before and nobody had complained. But the white Evangelical Church in the United States had shifted dramatically in the intervening years. While it had been slowly moving toward the empire during the decades of the Reagan Revolution and the growth of the Moral Majority, by the Trump years it had been swept into the arms of that empire. It could no longer see its sin. It had replaced its God. It had been coopted and domesticated by the royal consciousness. It had exchanged the foolishness of the Gospel for the wisdom of the world, the Sermon on the Mount for the Constitution, its witness of love for a mantra of hate for the "other." Like so many pastors at that moment, I wondered if I could continue to minister in that context.[6]

"SOS" WALTER

In May 2020, in the midst of the COVID-19 pandemic I created a podcast entitled *A Church Dismantled—A*

Kingdom Restored that soon developed a sizable following. Part of my thesis was that until racism was dismantled, the white middle-class church in America would continue its decline. While many appreciated the message that God was behind the collapse of much of the American Church, others fiercely resisted. I reached out directly to Walter. "Professor Brueggemann, why is my message that God is dismantling or taking apart the church hitting so much resistance? Isn't this exactly what you described God did in 587 BCE?"

Walter's response was comforting and confirming. He described an American church that bathed in a privatized and individualist culture. A church that cannot think systemically about the rise and fall of systems, that does not consider the church as an organism, institution, or system subject to macro-level pressures, challenges, or opportunities. Churches that include openness to looking beyond one's personal relationship with Jesus are better able to consider the decline of institutions. He described a progressive church that recognized ahead of evangelicals that the political jig is up. Christendom has declined. He also pointed to Jesus's crucifixion as the ultimate dismantling of God's very self. Walter also reminded me that those on the margins or those who care about the marginalized have less stake in preserving a church that is coming apart. When I got off the call, I recognized the genius of what Brueggemann has been offering pastors and the church. Hope, grounded in the biblical text, that God has an alternative reality to the one that lies in front of us for those who are willing to lift our eyes to see and hear it.

A few hours later I emailed Walter. "I need a road map for how a pastor walks through the crises in the church these days. *The Prophetic Imagination* guided me fifteen years ago. Do you have a biography that might do the same for me personally—show me the way Home even as the church is being dismantled?" Walter replied that he did not. A few hours later I emailed again: "Can I write your story? I need a map and a guide just as pastors did in the 1960s and 1970s. You provided it then and we need something like that again." The next day Walter agreed. The date was February 24, 2022.

WRITING THE BIO

Thus began a five-month whirlwind of twenty-five Zoom calls with Walter and about the same number with scholars, family members, former students, and colleagues. When I approached him about a biography, he replied, "There is nothing interesting about my life." Of course, I knew better. It became my mission to investigate what was in the spiritual and biographical basement of Walter Brueggemann, which led to more than one hundred published books and hundreds of essays, sermons, reviews, and more. What made the man tick? Why did *The Prophetic Imagination* emerge when and as it did? Why does it have such staying power?[7]

As I interviewed folks, I kept getting unsatisfying answers. "He is just smart." "It's inexplicable." "He reads so much." "He has a photographic memory." "He just works so hard!" Many knew little of Walter's first twenty years, of his family history, and his spiritual or confessional life. I began to believe that answering my two questions would resolve many others that I and others had about this unusual man.

Professor Brueggemann has been given a gift that some never receive—the opportunity to look back from the latter part of one's days to assess, reevaluate, and articulate the past even while living fully in the present.

From the margins of life, we always see differently—and perhaps with greater clarity—the truth about where we've been and who or what has formed what we have become. While some of us have that chance, too many fail to take the time to look back. The gift that Walter has been given and has embraced now becomes a gift for all of us, as Walter reminisces, reflects, and clarifies where and who he has been and indeed is still becoming.

Some will learn things they did not know about Walter before. Some will argue that I got Walter wrong. Some will have experienced Walter differently than the subject in this book. At eighty-nine, Walter is perhaps seeing things and articulating them differently than earlier in life. He sees his horizon and knows he has nothing to lose by letting the chips fall where they do. We ought to all be thankful and strive to be as honest ourselves. My effort was to read Walter as he read the biblical text and to stay within the bounds of that text, to treat Walter at eighty-nine as the ethnographic present from which I must observe and understand and articulate. I have sought to exegete Walter's life as he exegeted the biblical text. Make historical connections. Add sociological context. Add theology.[8]

Divided into three parts, this biography is couched within the theological frame of Jesus's parable of the soil, seed, and sower in Matthew 13. Part I of the book takes a deep dive into the "socially constructed world" into which Walter was dropped at birth, perhaps the most significant knowledge gap in all that is known about Walter's life to date. The central questions of this first part are: What was the nature of the cultural, sociological, historical, and religious soil that gave way to the prophetic imagination of Walter Brueggemann and became such a significant landmark throughout his life—one that he returned to time and again? What was the "prophetic habitat" of Walter's socialization within the German Evangelical Synod of North America tradition that produced one of the most prolific and influential theologians of the twentieth century? Why did Walter's pastor father so profoundly influence his youngest son? At the same time, what choices did Walter make that contributed to the soil's capacity to produce such an imagination?[9]

The second part of Walter's biography has to do with the nature of the seed that he carried and sowed across his life. What were the qualities of that prophetic seed or word that he so generously sowed among pastors, students, colleagues, and friends—not to mention the academy, church, and world? To answer this question, I will consider significant pivots throughout Walter's life—each an additional step in his own Exodus from moralism to freedom.

The third part of this book considers the worlds into which Walter Brueggemann—who many consider a modern-day prophet in the image of Jeremiah of old—sowed the seed he carried. Here again, we see how unpredictable and resistant to categories both Walter's life and work are, as we ask: Is he a scholar or church stateman? Is he a prophet or pastor? Is he in the world or the church? Is he at rest or restless? Is he for ecumenism or so critical of the contemporary church as to make ecumenism impossible? Is he revising his personal history or clarifying what so many of us had missed earlier? Is he a poet or a philosopher? Who changed the most in the last seventy years—Walter or the church?

Sometimes the veil lifts enough to make us think we know the answer, and Walter pivots again. Sometimes we think we understand his point, and then he offers a counterpoint. Just when we feel oriented by words of comfort and hope, we are suddenly thrust into disorientation, and our hearts are filled with doubt and fear. And then again, the clouds lift and we find ourselves suddenly in what appears to be a new space but perhaps is really the same old space for which we now have a new orientation.[10]

THE CONTRIBUTION

This book is not an effort to interpret everything that Walter has written. Many better qualified than I are doing so and will do so for decades to come. Instead, I intend with a broad stroke to paint the landscape into which Walter was born and out of which a prophetic imagination emerged, and how the carrier of that imagination propagated it across much of the twentieth-century church. To do this, we will observe Walter in the landscape of Blackburn, Missouri, and within the German Evangelical Pietism of his family and community. We will see Walter as a student at Elmhurst College, Eden Theological Seminary, and Union Theological Seminary. Finally, we will trace the movements of Walter as scholar, writer, teacher, mentor, preacher, and pastor to pastors, always responding in ways that analyze, sustain, construct, and renovate the worlds in which he lives and works.[11]

We observe Walter Brueggemann's energy, motivation, prophetic imagination, and pivoting here and there, emerging from God's world, a world that Walter would be the first to observe is the only world and the one world that includes all of the others in which both he and we find ourselves. The remarkable integration of Walter Brueggemann's life lies, as it can for any of us, in a life integrated with the biblical text and the God who is alive within that text.

What does this biography contribute to understanding the life and work of Walter Brueggemann? Few know much of the first twenty years of Walter's life. This biography will shed new light on Walter's early formation. I have relied upon rich archival and historical material to shape a cultural and historical narrative within which Walter's story belongs, but that has been unknown to most and even, to some extent, Walter himself.

This book is a look into Walter's inner life with God, searching for the answer to what of divinity has produced and sustained the quality and quantity of Walter's work. In interviewing even those who know Walter well, most claimed little knowledge or understanding of the nature of Walter's spirituality. It wasn't that folks doubted its existence, but no one could exactly identify what it was. It didn't fit standard categories. I have made an effort to address this question and am grateful for Walter's transparency and patience as we delved into his heart.

One of the least well-known gifts of Walter among his readers is the poetic prayers that he wrote before each class and then opened class by reading. Were these prayers the only published writing Walter had done, he would be widely recognized for these alone. But the massive contributions of other forms of writing have left these prayers primarily hidden. My view is that over time they will be seen as a rich contribution to Christian mystical literature, and of all Walter has written, they most reveal the rich spiritual soil and "life with God" out of which everything else that Walter wrote emerged. At my request, Walter has written nine original prayers for this book based on key passages that I lean upon throughout the book.

If all "theology is biography," as Walter states, then we have missed perhaps half of the story by not knowing more of Walter's rich personal and spiritual life. This biography not only takes a long view of that life but also dives deep into the community within which that life was lived, interviewing individuals who knew Walter over the decades. As much as this is the story of Walter Brueggemann, it is also the story of the community that he so intentionally engaged with, nurtured, and often led. This biography places Walter within the thick community in which he was formed as a child but which he always appears to be recreating wherever he goes. The integration of Walter's work and life within the context of his community across nine decades reveals the most complete understanding to date of this remarkable prophet, pastor, preacher, teacher, and friend.[12]

Walter's presence in looking over my shoulder as I wrote has strengthened the validity of this book. His has been a gentle presence, permitting me much grace and latitude to tell his story. I've had the great advantage of hearing what others have said about Walter and questions they have raised and then being able to ask, "Walter, is that really what you meant?," or "Could you clarify the interpretation that 'so and so' has made of your work?," or "What do you really think about 'this or that?'" Walter's response was often one of two: "Yes, that sounds about right," or "No, but here is what I meant or what I said!" As Walter notes, he is among the last of his generation in Old Testament study remaining, and Walter's presence in this book will be amply experienced by the reader. For, after all, this is a book about Walter.

I have tried to do a kind of hermeneutical exercise on Walter's life, in the same way that he did upon the text for so many decades. One of the great gifts that Walter has offered is that of interpretive and heuristic tools and typologies that bring the Bible to life and create new lenses through which to see what is happening in the text and with and by the God of that text. As I interviewed Walter, I would from time-to-time frame questions by using the same language back upon Walter that he had used on Jeremiah, Isaiah, or the psalmist. I found that doing so produced the richest insights, as Walter responded to language with which he was most comfortable and familiar.

Still, after all the work and careful research, and attentive listening, I don't pretend to have captured nearly all of who Walter Brueggemann is. As a biographical subject, he rejects reductionist portraits of himself, just as he rejects reductionism of the biblical text and the God of that text. For one who embraces typologies that have served his interpretive work so effectively, he also recognizes that typologies, or "ideal types" in the words of sociologist Max Weber, are imperfect. Walter is grounded deeply in the reality that worlds we have made and continue to make are messy, perhaps because he also sees the God who oversees those worlds as a bit messy. A God who cannot be fully measured, a God who pivots just when we imagined we knew where God was going, and a God whose mystery and preference for openness and unpredictability are enough to keep any one of us on our toes.

Others before me of course have written about the significance of *The Prophetic Imagination*, and others will do so long after me. Walter's dear friend and colleague Sam Balentine attributed the following words to Walter thirty-five years after the publishing of *The Prophetic Imagination*: "If today we ask where is the kingdom scribe who serves the secret of God, who risks standing at the pivot point between old and new without yielding to the seductions of either, then surely we must give thanks for Walter Brueggemann, who for so long has embodied a faithful response to this challenge. For your work, Walter, and for your dear friendship now over many decades, the words 'Thank you' are woefully inadequate."[13]

ACKNOWLEDGMENTS

I owe so much to so many people for their assistance and support. Walter's family and former colleagues and students especially caused me to feel included in a community that dearly loves the man. Those I interviewed included: Dr. Erskine Clark, Columbia Theological Seminary; Scott Holl, Eden Theological Seminary Archives; Dr. Christine Roy Yoder, Columbia Theological Seminary; Dr. Kathleen O'Connor, Columbia Theological Seminary; Rev. Clover Reuter Beal, Montview Avenue Presbyterian Church; Dr. Timothy Beal, Case Western University; Dr. Brent Strawn, Duke Divinity School; Mr. James Brueggemann, Dr. John Brueggemann, Skidmore College; Dr. Louis Stulman, Findlay University; Dr. Ellen Davis, Duke Divinity School; Rev. Dr. David Stabenfeldt; Rev. Roger Greene, St. Timothy Episcopal Church; President Deborah Krause, Eden Theological Seminary; Rev. Marc Nelesen, Third Reformed Church; Dr. Tod Linafelt, Georgetown University; Dr. Rolf Jacobson, Luther Theological Seminary; Dr. Douglass Meeks, Vanderbilt University; Dr. Jim Wallis, Georgetown University; Dr. Steve Nolt, Elizabethtown College; Rev. Dr. Patrick Keifert, Luther Theological Seminary; Dr. Christina Bucher, Elizabethtown College; and Dr. Clint McCann, Eden Theological Seminary.

I wish to acknowledge the Columbia Theological Seminary archivist Caitlin Greeves Greenamyer and students Elliott Trojanowski and Mark O. Ong'ingo for digitizing my requests for materials from the Brueggemann archives; The Young Center for the Study of Anabaptist and Pietist Groups of Elizabethtown College for my appointment as a center fellow for summer 2022; student assistants Erin Vago and Claudia Mendez-Sanchez; and Elizabethtown College for their tremendous and unqualified support across the last three decades of all my various research pursuits. A more supportive scholarly context I couldn't have found anywhere else.

I particularly appreciate the important contribution of the Rev. Dr. Samuel Wells for reading and commenting on an early draft of the manuscript, and for the Foreword to the biography that sets up what is to come so perfectly. Thanks too for reviews of the manuscript by Dr. Samuel Balentine, president of Eden Seminary, Dr. Deborah Krause, Dr. Kathleen O'Connor, Rev. Roger Greene, and Mike Schwartz.

I especially thank my dear wife Heidi for her unending support and unwavering confidence in my efforts to complete this project and so many others. The timeframe was short, and she was generous in granting me the space to complete the bulk of the writing during this summer. Her words of encouragement enabled me to push on, and her comforting presence sustained me.

The book owes much to the editorial efforts of Dr. Carey Newman, executive editor at Fortress Press, who showed me a new way to write and freed me from many of the habits that I thought led to good writing. Carey is excellent at his craft, and I am so fortunate he ended up at Fortress Press just before this book project began.[14]

And of course, this book would remain unwritten had Walter Brueggemann not permitted this stranger (as I was to him at the time), from interrogating relentlessly the sociological basement of his life. Our weekly

sessions were such a joy for me. I anticipated them,
knowing that I was a very fortunate seminary student
indeed, in conversation one-on-one with one of the
leading theologians of the late twentieth century.

As I conclude this prelude to Walter's story, I do
so by sharing one of nine prayers that Walter has written to accompany this book. The following is based on
Matthew 13 and reflects the overarching metaphor for
this book: Walter the sower—a prophetic imagination
the seed, and we the soil that receives the seed.

The Sower Who Seeds the New Kingdom

You are the sower of seeds among us:

> The seeds you plant are so small that we do
> not notice their offer of mercy;
> The seeds you plant are so tiny that we do
> not observe their gift of forgiveness;
> The seeds you plant are so minuscule that we
> do not heed their summons to justice.

And we—we are the soil that may receive the seeds you
sow:

> Some days we are bird-infested;
> the predators come and take the seed
> before we have a chance,
> they fly away, and we are left seedless.
> But not every day!
> Some days we are rocky, unreceptive soil,
> hard-nosed, cynical, indifferent, and the
> seeds have no chance with us.
> But not every day!
> Some days we are soil filled with thorns that
> are prickly and hostile,

choking off your seeds of compassion,
>   giving them no chance to sprout.
But not every day!
Some days we are good soil,
>   We have no predatory birds in our midst;
>   We have no choking resistance;
>   We have no prickly thorns on our
>   persons;
We receive the seed of your kingdom with
>   welcome.
We host your seed of mercy and compassion
>   and justice;
>   they sprout among us, and we see the
>   growth of your neighborly kingdom.
>   Not every day . . . but some days:
>   some days ready;
>   some days fertile;
>   some days receptive,
>   ready for mercy, fertile with compas-
>   sion, receptive to justice.
Lord of all our days and governor of all our
>   times, let this day be such a day for us.
We will gladly receive the seed you sow;
We see it grow into wellbeing.
We will be grateful;
We will sing praise, and be glad that we
>   could be hosting soil for your gracious
>   newness.
Amen.

Conrad L. Kanagy
Elizabethtown, Pennsylvania
August 8, 2022

PART ONE

ONE

A Prophetic Breakthrough

*It was more of a breakthrough than I understood
at the time.*

Walter Brueggemann

He was anxious. It was two o'clock in the afternoon.
By now, this was supposed to be his time—two
to five o'clock. Everybody in the office knew the drill.
But the questions kept coming. Next weekend's board
meeting agenda? The new hire who needed to be oriented? The never-ending enrollment concerns? The
UCC denominational executives arriving tomorrow?
Walter wondered why so much got pushed down to his
office. The short answer? Everyone knew that whatever
ended up on the dean's desk always got done—typically
before it was due. Amid all the questions, he responded
graciously to the secretary, who appeared beleaguered
by the assault on his time. He knew none of this was
her fault.

Suddenly he left the office. What remained undone
would remain for tomorrow. The thing that couldn't
remain another moment was his writing. The seminary
would survive without him in that office one more minute. But he wasn't sure he would survive if he stayed. Soon
his energy returned. The change in his pace reflected

the change in his mood. He bounded up the stairs of the dining hall to the building's second floor. His anxiety began to wane as he turned the key. Opening the door to the tiny hideaway office that few knew about, he went immediately to his desk. Finally, finally, those coveted and uncoerced moments of emancipation! The moments he lived for. Serving as dean was just the price he paid for this time. Commitment to Eden Seminary, the only seminary of his childhood faith tradition, was a cost he was willing to pay. After all, they had generously and patiently seen that his struggling father got through decades before.

The hideaway was his haven, maybe even a bit of heaven. If Jesus needed to get away for God's sake, the Almighty understood that the dean of a seminary did too, especially when so much of the work didn't seem that much about Jesus. While some faculty used their hideaway offices to nap between classes, Walter used his to finally awaken. They were restored by sleeping—he by writing. He had little time for sleep at all, let alone in the middle of the afternoon when he could be at his desk. Alone. Gloriously alone, except for his library and the biblical text. Oh yes, and that free God of the text. A monk, the students called him. He received that as a compliment.

He began to write even before removing his coat. He wrote long-hand, always his preference—pen to paper. And as on most days, he knew exactly where to begin. Throughout the day he had mentally mapped out his work for the afternoon. He often escaped into his writing, even if only in his head and not in his hideaway. He had the remarkable capacity to unplug from whatever else he was doing to plug back into his writing. His capacity to do so was growing by the day. Isolated from others, he could focus on the subject matter at hand. Some days he would break for a short game of basketball with the male students who loved when he joined them. The problem was that he was as fierce and determined on the hardwood as he was at the blackboard. And in both contexts, he was determined to win at all costs. More than one student had paid the price for getting in his way. But no basketball today—he had gotten to the hideaway late.

Walter was among friends in the hideaway, with his library around him and the books needed for that afternoon's work spread out on his desk: the biblical text first and foremost, Norman Gottwald, Peter Berger, Gerhard von Rad, José Miranda, Abraham Heschel, Robert Friedrichs, and a host of commentaries. Still, he knew his most extensive library was in his head—always had been. Walter read more books in a week than most faculty did in a month. He also read across disciplines, always curious about what those in other fields were saying, and always read one or more national newspapers daily.

On a good day, he produced the equivalent of twelve pages, typed double-space in two or three hours. He had many good days. The next morning he dictated the written work and handed it to his secretary. She deciphered between the handwriting and dictation and delivered it back to him as cleanly typed text that he rarely edited. He figured that he usually got it right the first time.

MAKING CONNECTIONS

He clearly had a remarkable gift with words. He had long been able to connect words in the biblical text that brought the Bible to life along with its God. Walter had—at least implicitly—assumed the mantle of Professor James Muilenburg, his Doctor Father at Union

Seminary. Like Muilenburg, he was a powerful presence in the classroom as he acted out the characters of the biblical text. He mimicked their voices as he roamed the room, all in the service of illustrating his exegetical method that combined the critical rhetorical method of Muilenburg with an interpretive social science approach. He called it post-critical. Whatever it was, he had moved far beyond the historical-critical method that still held sway in biblical studies. In his mind, that earlier mode was moribund and had little to offer the church or its pastors. The biblical text was a living document that told the story of a living God who related to a living people past and present. He had perfected the technique of making these connections in the text and then adding the lens of sociology before adding theology. The biblical text was meant to be a free document that told the story of a free God who related to a free people past and present. Life and freedom—those were words he was learning to live by the longer he wrote.

Students with little background in the Old Testament suddenly found themselves drawn in a magical way to words that had seemed foreign and alien before. Walter's pedagogy readily crossed the line into preaching, and, in fact, many of his students were converted to some subfield of biblical studies. He had an uncanny ability to see who was responding to his altar call and who was not. For those who were, he did not hesitate to demand that they walk the sawdust trail to conversion. Sometimes he called them out in public: "You will be an Old Testament theologian" or "you will be a pastor." Students of nominal faith or who had little idea about the Bible but had somehow stumbled into seminary fell spell to his teaching. To their amazement, they found the Bible interesting. The next thing they knew, Walter had changed their lives forever.

Students endowed Brueggemann with rock star status: "Dr. Brueggemann kicks ass!" and "He is just so freaking smart on his feet talking; it is incredible what comes out of his mouth." They kept lists of the top ten one-liners from their courses: "The Old Testament just keeps jerking you around," and "The church is a cottage industry for denial," and "Apocalyptic doesn't make any sense to people who are tenured!" Little was sacred in the classroom, and everything was up for discussion. At the same time, everything was sacred. God was going to judge the royal empire. The domesticated text was set free. The high-browed academic–industrial complex with its own royal consciousness would be laid low. Students had never heard this stuff in Sunday School. The truth was most of them couldn't remember much of Sunday School at all. But this was drama. This was cosmic theater. This would keep them awake for a lifetime! Even an eternity perhaps.

Because the beauty of the text drew him to the Old Testament, it drew them. Because he loved the text, they loved it. Because it spoke to him, it spoke to them. Because he loved the God of the text, they came to love that God. The loftiness and mystery of the words describing the "otherness" of God created new riddles about the Almighty, the unpredictable and free-roaming YHWH who declared a "full end" to a rebellious people and then called the full end off in the next breath (Jeremiah 4:27). Texts like this challenged their belief in God's changelessness. Walter debunked the idea that scribes had messed with the text in this case. Why couldn't the Almighty do what the Almighty wanted to do? Students who had grown up believing in the omniscience of God now began to see that God had been trapped by their theology. A God behind bars was no God at all. Neutered and domesticated was the God they had known prior to Walter. Full of life and free to roam was the God they knew after Walter.

SIGNS OF CHANGE

The year was 1977. Walter was feverishly working on a new project for which he still had no title. He only knew that the book was bringing together novel thoughts and intersecting ideas that were merging like a perfect storm. Whether the storm would erupt in a cloudburst or pass quietly by remained to be seen, but he had high hopes for the book. Whether the sacred words would break into the everyday realities of the tumultuous 1970s— the aftermath of the civil rights movement; the push for equality for women; protests about the Vietnam War and scared draft dodgers in his classes; the institutional crisis of Watergate; the burgeoning gay rights movement—he wasn't sure. But his words seemed to capture something both old and new that was boiling within and around him. He didn't have a name for the swirling of the times, but the more hours he spent in the book of Jeremiah, the more he began to imagine that the same God had an alternative reality for the twentieth century other than the one that lay in front of them now. Perhaps God was thrusting that very vision upon Walter.

What he did know was that he seemed to be seeing and experiencing something new and refreshing and emancipating in the text. The text just kept opening up new possibilities for God's governance in the world. Maybe a divine response was still in the works to address the crises of the 1960s and 1970s—chaos, pessimism, and disillusionment with society and its institutions, including the church. Walter's fresh reading of the Old Testament text opened his imagination to new possibilities about God's answers to the chaos. He didn't see it all very clearly at the time, but like the prophets of old who experienced God as a real agent who held out promises and hope, so Walter began to see his own work from that kind of perspective. Was he a prophet? The thought unnerved him. He only knew that he was beginning to see the world in a brighter light within the dimness of his hideaway office. He was coming to sense the grandeur of God within the smallness of that space. He was starting to experience the freedom of God within the confines of that little hideaway.

Like Jeremiah of old, Walter knew that he was called not only to "build up" but also to "tear down." Just as Jeremiah's enemies accused him of a double-tongue or a bifurcated mind that couldn't make itself up, so did Walter's detractors. "Gnostic" some called him.[1] A neo-Marxist. A liberal hack. A heretic. Interested only in social justice but not Jesus. However, Walter saw himself as a loyal critic of the church—one who also deeply loved the church. After all, the church was the only carrier of the only Story that mattered, and where the church existed faithfully the marginalized and poor received care. But how would the church be reformed if it failed to address its tendency to be autonomous from God? If it failed to confront the world of violence and predation and greed inside and outside the church?

WRITING DELAYED

Walter graduated from Union Seminary in 1961 and came directly to Eden Seminary as a faculty member. Eden was home. It was the seminary of the Evangelical Synod of North America in which he had been raised. His father, who never completed high school, graduated from Eden at a time when such a thing was possible. The patience of the faculty with his father's academic struggles had endeared the school to Walter. Following an undergraduate sociology degree at Elmhurst College, Walter attended Eden for his MDiv. When invited to return as a Professor of Old Testament Theology, the decision was a no-brainer. He would give back to the church what it had given to his father, August. He would give back to future pastors on behalf of his father. Perhaps he could save them from the abuse his dad had experienced in ministry.

Seven years passed before he published his first book. Until 1978, he would publish just five others.[2] This was an adequate, even exceptional number for Eden Seminary faculty and more than Walter had anticipated. At Union Seminary in New York City, no one emphasized the importance of research and scholarly publication. No one set him on a research agenda. He had no mentors besides his father, who knew nothing of writing and publishing. His inferior childhood education, the reality of his father's struggles in seminary, and the distance he felt between himself and those at more prestigious institutions all led to a deep sense of humility. He doubted he had the tools or skillset to become a widely recognized author, but he read voraciously across disciplines and was always curious about possible connections between one thing and another. And he worked like a beaver![3]

His efforts at writing in any fuller way were delayed for nearly a decade. In 1968, when he was still the junior faculty member at Eden, two faculty peers approached him in his office. His colleagues presented Walter with a written petition from the entire faculty body, restless with a need for fresh administrative leadership of the academic program. In a decade when seminaries were

declining and closing at an alarming rate, somebody
needed to be at the helm. Walter himself was so concerned about the possibility of Eden Seminary shutting
down that he enrolled in a PhD program in education
at St. Louis University. Eden faculty were divided about
how to move forward in the changing ecclesial and social
climate. The last major decisions about curriculum revi-
sion had occurred under Richard Niebuhr's watchful
eye. He had modernized the curriculum, bringing in
the social and behavioral sciences. The fact that a phil-
osophically divided faculty had all settled on Walter to
be dean said something about this young man's capaci-
ties for creating functional learning communities.[4]

He was surprised by the faculty's confidence in him,
unsure of what they saw in the youngest of the faculty
members. Perhaps it was his German work ethic or the
fact that he genuinely admired and got along well with
his colleagues. Perhaps it was his deep roots at Eden. He
had planned to teach pastors, not manage colleagues.
The task of supervising peers felt daunting, but having
been asked, he agreed. Saying yes was in his bones and
the capacity to turn things around in his blood, and
Eden had formed both him and his father, as well as his
older brother, Edward. Eden was the only original seminary in the relatively small Evangelical Synod of North
America. If it closed, where would the next generation
of pastors come from? Would the German pietist tradition of his childhood be swallowed up by the strong
pull to assimilate with a broader American Protestantism that was already in full swing?

Walter's people had come to Missouri from
Germany in the mid-nineteenth century. It was still
the American frontier with the Louisiana Purchase just
thirty years prior. They were a people formed by the
Prussian Union that brought together Calvinist and

Lutheran congregations as one governmental body. Tired of conflicts and quarrels, they came committed to minimizing differences. They emphasized love for God and neighbor. Their first pastors were missionaries from German and Swiss free church mission stations. They brought their German evangelical pietism and irenic posture. "In all things charity," they declared. "Just love God and neighbor," they echoed. It was a rich and unusual ethos. Everybody at Eden knew that if one person could simply keep from messing things up even further, it was "WB." Thus he had little choice but to take up the position of dean. The one perk—he finally received a secretary, which would make a profound difference in his writing productivity down the road.

There was much in the dean's role to occupy his time and energy. Eden Seminary had been without a dean since Richard Niebuhr's tenure thirty years before, and the lack of leadership in the role was taking its toll on the seminary. Once Walter accepted the position, the current president's subdued manner meant that the faculty leaned heavily on their beloved dean. He was confidential and trustworthy. He rewarded excellence with notes of appreciation tucked into their mailboxes. He showed up at colleagues' lectures no one even knew he was aware of. He paid attention to their publications and conference presentations. He treated newly appointed faculty as if they had been seminary colleagues for years. He sacrificed what he was due if it helped them out. He was the last to leave the seminary each day. His evaluations were formative, not punitive. He wanted everyone to prosper. Then the seminary would prosper. And he hired a remarkable group of faculty in biblical studies—an extraordinary collegium for a seminary with such humble beginnings.[5] The only nagging catch was that the president needed to figure out how to relate to a dean he had not appointed or nominated. And yet, like everyone else, the president knew that his longevity in the role was owed to his overworked, well-liked dean of the faculty. And so the system just kept inching forward.

Even as dean, Walter taught a full load of three courses each semester, typically in the morning. He was known for his "alchemy" in the classroom. Like his teacher at Union, James Muilenburg, he merged performance art with a summons to bring forward a student's passion for the text. He was famous among students for jumping up on tables, mimicking the Almighty, and doing just about anything to help students make connections with the text. Sometimes the line between Walter and Jeremiah appeared very thin indeed. Before every class, Walter walked to his typewriter and tapped out a prayer for the class that was about to begin. He opened with a prayer invoking God Almighty or lamenting some injustice in the world. Then he lectured, and before long a stream of profanity erupted. Whatever it took to awaken the sleeping masses to the amazing mysteries of the text and the text's God.

Walter taught from the chalkboard. He sketched the word patterns of the text using the rhetorical analytical mode he learned from Muilenburg. He mapped for the students in Hebrew the patterns of repetition, parallelism, and advancement. He pointed out how words in the text carried a phrase. He focused on these words and cross-referenced them with their other usages in Scripture. It was as if he carried commentaries and Bible dictionaries and concordances between his two ears! Then he just drilled and drilled and drilled. He wanted them to know that they could do this kind of analysis too. On the one hand, his method seemed so sure and almost scientific. On the other, he reminded the students not to look for logical conclusions. Don't close the text—keep it free. Bind the text and you bind the God of the text. Historical criticism had had its day in the sun but yielded less and less light. It was a new day to let in the true light and stand by the real fire. Some called what Walter did rhetorical analysis, others said it was social science. Still others, including Walter, called it post-critical. And probably some thought it was simply voodoo. But those who listened deeply began to see less dimly, experience greater freedom, and feel strangely warmed.[6]

NEW ENERGY

As Walter sat writing on that afternoon, the administrative demands of the day quickly receded. As always, he quickly entered the text where he had stopped the day before. The pen and paper were like old friends who picked up the conversation as if it had never ended; because in fact, it had not. Keeping conversations going was essential to Brueggemann, whether with students, colleagues, family, the biblical text, or the God of that text. It's how worlds were made—with God and with others. That same kind of dialogic engagement was always happening with his manuscript as well. He had learned to track two conversations at once in his head—during those meetings with the president, listening to colleagues' complaints, or taking out his frustration through his evening run. Always channeling the text. Always in dialogue with God. Always imagining the next sentence. Even while responding to the president with "I will get on that immediately." And of course, he did. But he was at the same time two sentences further down the road of the manuscript by the time whatever the president had wanted was complete. The advantage of Walter's hobby was that time he could always carry it with him. And it always restored him.

Because the conversation never stopped in his head, with the text and the God of that text, writing was less like creating than simply responding to those ongoing conversations. Walter didn't need time to think about what to write. What he wrote had already been thought about at least at three levels—in dialogue with himself, the biblical text, and the God of that text. He never did quite understand his proximity to the divine word or the mystical nature by which inspired prayers bubbled up within him.

But there were also his students and colleagues— they were also engaged in these ongoing conversations. And then there was the breadth of interdisciplinary literature that increasingly entered these internal conversations pouring out through the pen. His mind acted as an intersection of an unlikely cast of characters, who were forced to hang out together in the same space, yielding all of those amazing one-liners and rich insights. In Walter's head, enemy concepts met for happy hour and found they were better together than apart. Writing was a series of encounters at one intersection after another. Marx met Jesus. Von Rad met Muilenburg. Barth met Berger. Childs met Ricoeur. Gottwald met Freud. Brueggemann met Fretheim and Childs. And what fun they all had together!

Brueggemann was nearing his twelve-page goal for the day and was getting close to the end of his three-hour block. He had not stood up for three hours and still wore his coat. He always eyed the clock with dread as the end drew near. One more new thought had just come. One more minute to get it out. And that thought was followed by another—that one could be tomorrow's first sentence. Would he forget until the next day? Unlikely. But he had to stop. He had promised the secretary one last check-in before she left. He had some final documents to sign. He always left last. And he knew James, his oldest and with his father's work ethic, was at home waiting to throw the football.

Walter recognized he was lucky to have stumbled onto work that he loved. As a kid, he baled hay, plowed corn, raked hay with horses, and worked at the Skelly service station, where he changed truck tires, sometimes in zero-degree conditions. He knew then what he did not want to spend his life doing. And watching the abuse his father experienced at the hands of congregational boards and church members, he also suspected that local congregational ministry was outside his call— seminary attendance or not. But nothing had prepared Brueggemann to be the scholar he was slowly becoming.

He still didn't think of himself in that light, sixteen years after becoming a seminary professor. He was a member of the Society for Biblical Literature (SBL), attended national meetings, and read Old Testament scholarship.[7] But he was more an observer than a participant and more a bystander than a contributor. The feeling was not unfamiliar. He was on the periphery in high school, where his closest friend was his older brother Ed. He had felt similarly at Union Seminary, with New York so far from the cornfields of Missouri and everybody else smarter and richer and more good-looking. And he had the same familiar feeling at the SBL. But amid his gratitude that he had escaped milking cows and changing tires, he realized that he still worked with the steel intensity of the farmers and mechanics he had grown up around. His work ethic, and his hand-to-the-grindstone approach to work, all revealed his family's recent immigrant status and his small-town origins.

Little did Walter understand that afternoon, writing in his hideaway, that his status at Eden Seminary, among scholars and in the broader church, was about to change. Previously, he had squeezed into the back of standing-room-only ballrooms to hear renowned scholars at the annual SBL meetings. Before long, he would be behind the lectern at the front, watching others shove their way into his own standing-room-only lectures. Walter's world would be transformed in unimaginable ways that he would welcome and sometimes want to flee.

CHILDHOOD

He was glad for the approaching affirmation and admiration. For fleeting moments it reminded him of what he had overcome—a poor educational background and marginalization as a pastor's child. In the German communities of Missouri, the pastor was always an outsider and never welcomed entirely into the network of families. The Brueggemann family of four was very tight, forced to rely on each other for support. Pastor tenures were ordinarily two to five years, and this made close community connections tentative and difficult to sustain. Members needed their pastor to be distant. When they required his ministry, they wanted a pastor, not a friend.

Walter's childhood marginalization was twofold. He was on the periphery within a thick German subculture that was itself peripheral to the larger American society following World War I. And being German during World War II didn't help matters. But marginality created fertile soil for him to begin to imagine another's world. How do others live? How do others spend their time and money? What do others believe? Tucked securely in the center of the dominant culture with greater security and certainty, his imagination would have atrophied. Had the American status quo been normative, he would have had little motivation to imagine an alternative reality. The center is too comfortable. Novelty is a threat, and otherness is to be feared.

There was much, however, to encourage Walter to engage his imagination besides his marginalization. The St. Louis Cardinals were not far away and, from time to time, August Brueggemann loaded his family up in their old Chevrolet for an outing to Sportsman's Park to watch their beloved baseball team. This was a luxury that few others in Blackburn ever had a chance to enjoy. Ed and Walter loved these family road trips. They were a break from the isolation and parochialism of Blackburn, and instead of Harry Carey's booming voice on their transistor AM radio, they got to sing "Take Me Out to the Ballgame" for the seventh inning stretch.[8] Summertime also meant a two-week getaway to Hudson, Kansas, where Walter's mother came from. August Brueggemann spent the two weeks harvesting wheat to supplement his meager ministry salary, doubling his annual income as a result.

Since his childhood in Blackburn, Missouri, as the son of a poorly educated and poorly paid preacher, Brueggemann had been aware of this sense that he was always behind everyone else. With only thirty students in his high school and just one shelf of books that he read and read again, Brueggemann relied upon others to subsidize his meager educational opportunities. But the advantage of working from behind meant that Walter was always working on getting ahead. This trait was about to bear more fruit than he or anyone could imagine. A breakthrough of sizable proportions was just around the corner.

Walter's childhood position on the periphery opened up the possibility of freedom and emancipation that would eventually assist him in moving forward. He didn't have to be like every other schoolboy because he couldn't ever be one of them. He didn't have to be like every other biblical scholar who published not to perish because his audience would become the church. While he didn't know it, Walter had been imagining alternative worlds long before this day in 1977, as he sat writing in his hideaway office. He had not yet landed upon the term "prophetic imagination," but what he had in mind was an assumption that all social reality owes its origins to the freshness of the always generative power of the biblical text and of that text's God. To the emancipation found in that text's God. To the freedom and sovereignty of that God to intervene in the world when and how God chose to do so. The imagination Walter was formulating was not just any alternative view of reality, but a view grounded in the biblical text. He had little to do with other views of social realty on the Religious Left or Right. Thus, the lens of a prophetic imagination was already in place. Walter was now becoming aware of that imagination and finding words to describe it. Doing so, he would define the direction of the rest of his life.

TO UNION SEMINARY

The discovery of his voice came slowly. He was an introvert by nature. His poor education was a factor, and his family's poverty and isolation were another. The German communities of Missouri were divided between those of the Lutheran Missouri Synod, which held to the higher Scholasticism of German Lutheranism, and the Evangelical Synod of North America, whose pastors were derived from farmers, tradesmen, and generally from the working class. Walter grew up in the latter tradition and personally experienced the tension between the two faith traditions. When a new Missouri Synod pastor showed up in Blackburn, August Brueggemann paid him a visit. But the new Lutheran preacher refused to stand up and greet August or acknowledge his presence. August turned around and went home, again reminded that he came from a people who were not good enough. Not educated enough. Not devout enough. Not wealthy enough. Not godly enough. It didn't take long for Walter to internalize this stigma. In an interesting twist of fate, this same minister was called by the local school board to teach the Brueggemann brothers Latin, a request insisted upon by their father and the only time Latin was ever taught in the school. So in the end that same minister helped make the Brueggemann brothers smarter!

Walter came back to his alma mater—Eden Seminary—as a faculty member, with the primary purpose of training pastors. The choice to return was easy when a position opened. He was clearly recognized by now as a child of his tradition, with a rich contribution to offer back to that tradition. Deep within him was the connection to his pastor father. August Ludwig Brueggemann was convinced by a local family physician in Bland, Missouri, to leave farming and enter the ministry. But he had struggled every semester, threatening to leave the seminary. He was always coaxed back by a caring and compassionate faculty member, Allen Wehrli, Walter's teacher, and now his colleague. Watching his father's difficult educational rite-of-passage had been painful. Walter chose to expend his primary energies on behalf of the clergy because of his father.

He would have many audiences, but none would be as important to him as pastors and prospective pastors. Never far from Walter's heart and mind, August Brueggemann loomed large for his son. A small thin man, he was also physically quite strong, and his faith, energy, and courage matched his strength. Walter learned that sophistication and status were far less important than most cracked them up to be. And he also learned to smell out pretense, while most were still in amazement at the pretender.

It would take time for Walter to understand that his natural habitat was scholarship for the church. There were so many other distractions and seductions because he was gifted at many levels—as a teacher, preacher, administrator, and writer. He put too much energy into activities that kept him from writing, like that circus in the dean's office. But something was emerging from out of the heavens to create new clarity and direction. What had long resided within Walter was soon to reveal itself to both him and the world.

The step from Webster Groves, Missouri, as a graduate of Eden Seminary to Union Seminary on Broadway Street, New York City, was far greater than the geographic distance of 994 miles between the two. Walter was terrified of the city and deeply anxious about his success during his three years there. He feared his lack of Hebrew language skills would hurt his progress. He had been directed to Union by his Eden Seminary teacher, Lionel Whiston, whether because he knew Walter could not make it at Yale or Harvard or because Union was the only seminary not doing history and archaeology as the dominant modes of Old Testament study. Walter would have died from boredom at such places.

But those years at Union Seminary would set him in a direction that would make the emergence of *The Prophetic*

Imagination more likely three decades later. The most apparent catalyst for that direction was Brueggemann's Doctor Father Professor James Muilenburg, Professor of Hebrew and Cognate Languages at Union Seminary from 1945 to 1963. Muilenburg's often dramatic lectures from the Old Testament brought the text to life for his students. His method of exegeting the Scripture steered students away from the dominant mode of historical criticism that still reigned in theological studies. For Walter and other students of Muilenburg, such as Phyllis Trible and Norman Gottwald, rhetorical analysis permitted one to see the movement, openness, and aliveness of the Bible and then apply the text to the contemporary world. This made the prophetic books much more accessible to pastors in the mid-1970s struggling in the swirling aftermath of the dramatic social movements of the 1960s. Of all Muilenburg's well-known students, Walter applied the method of rhetorical analysis to the church more than any.

He had learned well from James Muilenburg, the father of rhetorical analysis, and his performances as a storyteller. The rhetorical analysis apparatus became and remained Walter's primary stroke whereby one studies the shape and genre of the text. Rather than rushing into the Scripture to make theological interpretations, he taught his students to walk around the images, signs, symbols, and words in the text. The outcome is not only a more useful interpretation but also emancipation. One is freed from preconceived theological outcomes and instead the text is allowed to have its own voice. Walter would learn later the similarities of this method to good rabbinic interpretation that lives with a text to see what emerges from it. Muilenburg was a friend of Jewish theologian and rabbi Abraham Heschel, who taught at the Jewish Theological Seminary of America across the street from

Union Seminary. It is no wonder that rabbinical interpretive methods were picked by Brueggemann at Union Seminary. In addition, Heschel was active in the civil rights movement of the time, and his work reflected his posture toward the reproduction of social justice.

Heschel broke the claim of the omniscience of God and showed that God comes from beneath up into the drama of creation. God's natural habitat is with the poor, the weak, and the vulnerable. God is inescapably an advocate for them, and stands against the force of wealth, power, and learning. As a result, *The Prophetic Imagination* would lay claim to a God who stands in solidarity with those on the bottom of the heap. The Old Testament book of Jeremiah was Muilenburg's specialty, and also became Walter's. Much of what would emerge as *The Prophetic Imagination* was clearly developing within Walter at Union Seminary. Watching Muilenburg, Walter came to understand that the character and the agency of God in the biblical text are real and not simply a human projection.

Across the next forty years, the major accent of his work would assume that God was a real agent and a lively character in the imagination of the biblical community. The problem with conservatives, Walter was learning, was the reduction of God's agency to a formula. They clung to predetermined categories constructed for an earlier day and hour. They created the same moribund text as did historical criticism of progressives, also offering little to the church and its pastors.

THE BREAKTHROUGH

The unexpected reception to *The Prophetic Imagination* would begin to chip away at Walter's insecurities and suggest that his doubts about himself might be faulty. The publication of this one book would catapult him to the foreground of biblical studies as one of the church's leading theologians. The publication of one book written in God's Kairos moment opened Walter's eyes to the fact that he could do scholarship for pastors in a way that no one else was doing—certainly not his scholarly colleagues at Harvard and Yale.

Regardless of the season of his life, he ministered to pastors through teaching, mentoring, writing, lecturing, leading pastor support groups, and preaching. But the manuscript he was writing now, while it would address the needs of pastors in a swirling society, would also catch the academy's attention and demand greater respect for Brueggemann's methodology for reading and interpreting the biblical text. Until *The Prophetic Imagination* became widely accepted, Walter had always considered himself a teacher to pastors.

The Prophetic Imagination's appearance in the 1970s is a mystery even to those closest to him, as is the answer to the question of just what "makes Walter Brueggemann tick?" Responses of "inexplicable," or "I've never thought about it," or "he reads so much outside of his field," or "he is just so damn smart" are typical. For many, the riddle of Walter Brueggemann remains unsolved. Most are so astonished by the quality and quantity of the man's work that the thought of how this all came to be is rarely uppermost in their minds. Why worry about the ingredients in the secret sauce as long as the sauce keeps making the cuisine taste so fine? Most are too much in awe to seriously imagine that an answer is discernible.

Interestingly, even among those who share Walter's faith commitments, few seem to consider that the Holy might be credited for what occurred in 1978 that changed everything. In other words, few apply to this prophet the tools of interpretation he so deftly applied to the biblical text and the prophets. Few imagine that turning a prophetic imagination upon the prophet himself might yield some answers. Few consider that the call and gifts of the prophets of old just might be expressed among them today in their professor, teacher, colleague, and dean.

But what would be seen and understood if the prophetic imagination were applied to Walter? What if the typologies others find helpful in interpreting the biblical text were layered onto Brueggemann's biography? And what if the possibility of the otherness of God that Walter credits to the Old Testament prophets were given even a bit of consideration in the secret sauce that makes him tick? What if it was God first and foremost who met him at the burning bush? Or called his name in the middle of the night? Or met him in the temple? Or called him as a child like Jeremiah?

The eruption of *The Prophetic Imagination* was a coming together of numerous factors in addition to the call of the Holy. Brueggemann's reading of Paul Ricoeur, a French philosopher who also dabbled in theology through a hermeneutical lens, led to a more "interpretive" approach to reading the Bible and a recognition of socially constructed realities of social life.[9] He combined this interpretive approach with the form of rhetorical analysis that was passed to him through Professor James Muilenburg of Union Seminary. Walter believed that not only was historical criticism a static method that confined God and "God's mighty deeds" to the text and the dustbin of history, but it was also useless in addressing the social chaos and psychological anxiety swirling in the wake of the civil rights movement, the women's liberation movement, the Vietnam War and subsequent protests, and the increasing disillusionment with society's institutions. Looking for theological and sociological answers, he began to immerse himself in the liberation theology of the 1970s, particularly José Miranda's writings. Where he picked up Miranda's book *Marx and the Bible* he doesn't remember. He does recall, however, that Miranda opened up a whole world about which he knew little previously. At the same time, he recognized in Miranda labels for concepts and realities that he knew intuitively to be true.[10]

Walter was particularly impacted by the insistence of Miranda in visiting and revisiting Jeremiah 22, where the prophet has God say, "to care for the poor and the needy, is this not to know me?" This was a crystalizing moment for Walter, as he recognized that the text did not say if one has knowledge of God, then they will care for the poor. Or that if one cares for the poor, they will get knowledge of God. Rather, it simply declares that "the care of the poor is knowledge of God." Knowledge of God is practice! That verse alone was a turning point for Brueggemann. Walter used Miranda's work to build upon his early personal sense of injustice on behalf of his father. While liberation theology was new to him, it struck him as so true. He knew that Miranda's was the direction without knowing entirely why. But he had come to understand that liberation was a tag word for what he was about and who he was, and the theme of deliverance was one that he would spend an enormous amount of energy on.

A sociology major at Elmhurst College when Émile Durkheim's structural-functionalist theories reigned in the discipline, Brueggemann, intentionally or not, followed the sociological shift from structural-functionalism as the leading paradigm in the first half of the twentieth century to conflict theories grounded in Karl Marx in the 1970s. Just as sociologists were abandoning structural-functionalism in their search for theories that predicted social inequalities by race, sex, and wealth, Brueggemann followed their lead in seeking to make the biblical text relevant to the same social dynamics in the church and the world.[11] But more than simply understanding for himself, Brueggemann was looking to offer hope to pastors who found themselves at theological places so different from their congregants on the social issues of the day. He created a way to theologically address the stirring within clergy around issues of justice; clergy who, because of the dominance of historical criticism in their theological training, did not have a framework for thinking critically and with relevance about these issues.

Some readers likely missed the driving passion for justice that marked *The Prophetic Imagination*, which would be a landmark of Brueggemann's work for the rest of his life. But the desire for justice was deeply personal, emerging in part from how poorly his dad was treated as a pastor. While his concern for justice, even as a teenager, was being shaped by more than his experience of injustice to his father, he internalized that experience such that he could readily apply it to others. Living out of the prophetic imagination continues to be a source of energy for pastors who can from time to time mobilize their courage for witnessing to a world other than the one that is in front of them.

Walter was growing in his recognition that he was a gifted writer. The reception of *The Prophetic Imagination* would strengthen this personal awareness. Still, up to this point, after sixteen years as a seminary professor and at forty-four years of age, he had not believed himself adequate for the task. While he actively participated in the SBL, he did not see himself as a scholar in his participation. But all of this would change with the publication of *The Prophetic Imagination,* which would sell more than one million copies. At future SBL meetings, Brueggemann would no longer find himself alone, but would be a central attraction at the book exhibit with groupies traipsing around after him.

The Prophetic Imagination was published in 1978, but it took several years before Brueggemann realized that he had hit a home run that would change his life and even his family forever. It was a happy time in the Brueggemann household, with Walter feeling good about *The Prophetic Imagination.* It certainly was not known yet what he would become, but by 1980 it had become clear that he had a talent for preaching and teaching and that a pipeline for writing was being dug.

The themes of the book reflected the pain, grief, and cries of the moment. In the wake of the Vietnam War, the United States was still picking up the pieces from a nation torn apart by division and conflict. The book was well received in part because no white theologian had done biblical interpretation for the contemporary white church in the same way before Brueggemann. Paul Ricoeur's idea of imagination as constructing a world other than the one that is in front of us struck a nerve among many people who knew that the church had to do things differently, but who, until *The Prophetic Imagination,* did not have a frame of reference for how to move ahead with such a project.[12]

Black theologians had long written of the kind of freedom and emancipation of which Brueggemann wrote. But the segregated nature of the Academy and church meant that these theologies were often unknown beyond the Black Church. The white church required a new language and the envisioning of an alternative reality for being the church in the world; *The Prophetic Imagination* offered just that. It revealed the relevance of the Scripture for contemporary realities by introducing an exegetical approach to the Bible that challenged the dominant historical-critical lens through which Scripture was being interpreted in the academy. Brueggemann began to recognize that historical criticism had little to offer the church. It had no energy and offered no hope of God's engagement with contemporary affairs. It was "moribund!" *The Prophetic Imagination* changed all that and would become the defining theological contribution of Brueggemann's life. While he would move from the book of Jeremiah to write about Deuteronomy, the Psalms, Isaiah, and more, the prophetic imaginative lens would continue to guide his interpretation of Scripture. And Walter has spent the past forty years articulating and applying that imagination to one text after another. By reading two or three newspapers daily and eight or nine books weekly, he never tired nor lost the capacity to apply that imagination to what God was up to in the contemporary world. Nor did he ever retire from confronting that world with prophetic truth that originated in his newly found voice of *The Prophetic Imagination*.

The naming of the book came at the last moment, and only later did Brueggemann learn that the phrase had come from a description of Flannery O'Connor's work.[13] He wished it had been his! It is no surprise that the two of them held "prophetic" and "imagination" together as both were pursuing a similar agenda. Both recognized that prophetic faith was flat without imagination. Bringing together "prophetic" with "imagination" also leads to poetic language that confronts oppressive powers. Both invoke Abraham Heschel. Both were concerned with false or royal consciousness.

While a prophetic imagination will be forever identified with Brueggemann, he was merely the willing scribe who so well captured the imagination available to anyone who approaches the biblical text with an honest heart and open ears and who truly believes that "the word of God is living and active and sharper than any two-edged sword, piercing until it divides soul from spirit, joints from marrow . . . able to judge the thoughts and intentions of the heart" (Hebrews 4:12). In this, there was little new about Brueggemann's prophetic imagination. It was a message from the ancient past embodied in the contemporary prophet who did not think of himself as extraordinary and saw himself as just the opposite. Brueggemann's willingness to defy the historical-critical method and accept the text as a living book from a residing God written for a living people with a living imagination accounts for God's ability to use this man in such remarkable ways. It may be possible for evangelicals with their closed categories to imagine again and progressives with their loss of any divine imagination to believe again.

The success of *The Prophetic Imagination* also required a readiness to receive such a message. Social movement theory predicts that folks are more likely to receive a message in soil that has been softened or cultivated by macro-level events that impact them personally. The turmoil of the 1960s prepared the church, but especially pastors, for a new and relevant word from God that would reveal where God's people had been in a similar place in the past and how God helped them get home. Without a new method of exegeting the Scripture beyond the static categories of historical criticism, there was little hope for returning to that path back home. Social change is also more likely where structural strain pushes folks to look for newly imaginative answers because the pain of not doing so is too great and creates too much anxiety. Repeated research from the 1960s consistently revealed that pastors were far more supportive of the civil rights movement than were their members. This clergy–member disagreement caused conflict in many congregations where the pastor's seminary experience had not prepared them for this level of congregational conflict and societal upheaval.

What did the Bible and the Bible's God have to offer the church now? Trained in historical criticism, most pastors assumed "not much." But a new answer was coming, in the form of "a prophetic imagination." *The Prophetic Imagination*'s publication in 1978 was a much-needed catalyst for change in the church to address society's suffering. It is not an overstatement to say that the prophetic imagination was the catalyst that moved the church out of the iron cage of Enlightenment rationalism that had infected both evangelicals and progressives—evangelicals with their closed categories and progressives with open categories but no God inside.

Brueggemann showed up just in time, preaching a text with imagination, a text that held within it a God with imagination, who invited God's people to use *their* imaginations to see an alternative reality to the one that was currently facing them. What was happening behind that hideaway office was more than book-writing. Instead, it was the meeting between God and his humble prophet who was never sure he had the goods to write and publish. Whether he did or not is now a moot point, since it is clear that the goods were given to him by Grace to a willing prophet who said, "Speak Lord, for your servant listens" (I Samuel 3:10).

That servant now recognizes, as do all who follow his lead, that a prophetic imagination is a way of listening to God that can be applied time and again to the text. It refuses closure and always speaks in multiple voices that require yet another interpretation. Every time one goes back to the text, it will yield something more. For the text cannot be reduced to a one-dimensional interpretation in any direction. It refuses alignment with pet projects or favorite mantras, and it always requires another formulation.

At the end of the day the text and its God must be emancipated.

> I think many people have formulated the notion that the freedom of God lives at the interface with the faithfulness of God. And the church always wants to stress the faithfulness of God and that you can count on God. But the freedom of God keeps subverting the faithfulness of God so that every time God exercises freedom, then God must reformulate the character of God's faithfulness, and I think that's an ongoing project. I have argued a time or two that God has a very unsettled interior life. And of course, this is great heresy in a church that doesn't want God to have that kind of unsettled quality.[14]

But, unquestionably, it is no more heretical than a prophetic imagination that takes God's people back to the Bible once again.

TWO

Where Prophets Come From

*My use of the term "evangelical" means those who
trust the Gospel as distinct from those who trust the
church. It really means confidence in the news of
the Gospel. Pietism emerged in Lutheranism to
escape the rationalistic dogmatism of the Lutherans.*

Walter Brueggemann

It was a typical Sunday morning in June as the sun
rose over Blackburn, Missouri. Walter, the youngest
of the two living Brueggemann sons, woke first. His
brother Ed invariably slept later if he could. Suddenly
remembering their discussion from the night before,
Walter elbowed his brother, "Come on, Ed, it's time
to get up! Remember where we're going to church—
we're skipping Dad's sermon this morning and going to
the Black church!" The boys had conferred with their
father August the evening before, and he had agreed
to their plan. After all, they had heard the sermon he
would preach the next day at St. Paul's Evangelical and
Reformed Church many times before, stirring the saints
to love God and their neighbor and somehow weaving
into the message the ills of ignorance and the importance of education. For a farmer turned preacher who
never finished high school and barely got through Eden

Seminary, August had reason to either ignore or eschew the topic of education in his sermons. He chose neither and instead consistently encouraged his flock to raise their eyes to the opportunities that education would offer their children during the Great Depression and World War II.

TO MISSOURI

August himself, who never completed high school, knew of what he spoke. His father, Frederick Wilhelm, had come to Missouri at fifteen years of age with the mass migration of Germans during the mid-nineteenth century. They came by the tens of thousands through New Orleans and up the Mississippi and Missouri rivers, settling in the rich river bottoms that reminded them so much of their fatherland. Establishing clusters of small German communities, they had come to the United States frontier for various reasons. Some came to escape the ongoing religious quarrels and conflicts between Lutherans and Calvinists. Despite the Prussian Union declared by Prince Frederick Wilhelm III in 1817 that forced a union of Lutheran and Calvinist congregations under one governing body, religious quarrels continued. Many pastors rejoiced in the new reality of unity as an alternative to their centuries-long conflicts. Others seemed to prefer the current reality of quarreling, cynical about a union created so the Lutheran prince could take communion with his Calvinist wife. Both groups migrated to Missouri at the same time and brought their differences to the American West's rapidly growing New Rhineland. One group would become the German Evangelical Synod of Missouri Lutheran and the other the German Evangelical Synod of the West.[1]

Johann Friedrich Wilhelm Brueggemann came perhaps to escape the church altogether. He was not alone. An entire group of German freethinkers went to the Midwest to shed the pressures of religious conformity and to freely express their irreligious views. Some were highly educated, and others were farmers and tradesmen with little education. Frederick Wilhelm Brueggemann fell into the latter group. From a family of pig farmers in Schleptrup, a village just outside Engter, Germany, he had been baptized in 1840 in a Prussian Union congregation. Frederick didn't consider himself a Christian—he was never convinced of religion's value, and it seemed to have brought more violence than peace to his homeland. He and everyone else in Germany remembered the stories of the Thirty Years' War between Calvinist and Lutheran traditions that were partly responsible for the death of one-half of Germany's population through war, famine, and disease. If anything, Frederick Wilhelm had come to escape wars—religious and otherwise. The appeal of natural religion that flowed from the Enlightenment kept calling to him, and perhaps the new lands just purchased from France a few decades earlier would offer what he was looking for. The only time that August remembered his father Frederick crying was as August set off for World War I, with Frederick uttering, "I left Germany so that there would be no more wars to fight."

Little did Frederick realize that in coming to Missouri he was about to enter the most violent and painful period in American history, as the South fought the North over the emancipation of Black slaves. And Missouri became one of the war's most divided and conflicted states. Frederick enlisted in his late teens or early twenties with a regiment from Missouri and made it safely through the war. Upon returning to his hometown, he eventually married Augusta Bueker, who, unlike her husband, had been born in Missouri and seems to have been a devout church member. She gave birth to eleven children, the two youngest being August and Albert. Both would become pastors in the German Evangelical Synod of North America, the church body descended from the Prussian Union of 1817. Trained as a blacksmith, August would take up farming like his father and eventually marry Hilda whose background was Swiss rather than German.

But this morning, like every other, the brothers had each other and the chance to join the small Black community of about thirty for worship, something none of their peers would ever chance to do. They dressed, ate, and walked together to the small church at the edge of town. While Walter remembers the service as relatively uneventful—the little congregation had no pastor of its own—their periodic visits were early acts of identifying with those on the margins—in this case descendants of slaves. This was the beginning of seeing the injustices that existed right in their little town where nearly everybody went to church and identified with the Christian faith. Perhaps their marginalization in Blackburn gave the boys freedom to step outside the constraints of conformity required of their peers—a freedom that is a prerequisite for any future prophet. But perhaps also it was an early glimpse for Walter of the many ways that the church is coopted and domesticated by the dominant culture.

The boys' father, August, had modeled crossing the "color line" by befriending the local Black schoolteacher, the type of relationship that few white pastors in rural communities like Blackburn were willing to engage in. Eventually, August was able to get a job for his boys as the custodians of the two-room elementary school for colored children (the high schoolers were bused out of town). Jim Crow was alive and real in Blackburn.

MISSIONARY PASTORS

As this religious and social mix of German immigrants entered the New World, it was not entirely clear how they would organize themselves religiously or to what degree the religious structures and values of the fatherland would accompany them to New Rhineland. Few churches existed, and none were German speaking. Longer established church leaders in the Northeast United States began to express concern about the possibility of conversion by the new immigrants to Roman Catholicism. New Rhineland was rife with Romanists trying to convert the new migrants and an appeal was made back to the fatherland. In response, mission houses from Basel, Switzerland, as well as Barmen and Bremen, Germany, began to discern a response to this looming crisis of identity and faith for the immigrants. But if and how to respond was not clear—was Missouri really a mission field? Were the German immigrants' pagan souls in need of salvation? How could the mission houses justify sending missionaries to the midwestern United States? Mission leaders finally agreed that the need met the necessary criterion, and so, more overtly than covertly, they began to train men to be pastors for the emerging communities of faith in Missouri.

While the Prussian Union had from the beginning been an ecumenical venture among two historically competing Protestant traditions, there was no guarantee that the congregations of this union would reflect the German pietism that emerged in the seventeenth and eighteenth centuries. But German mission houses were centers of pietism and had no formal ties to the church governance of the Prussian Union. Their early and robust presence among the immigrants in Missouri helped to assure that pietism's values found their way into the religious soil of the new churches emerging in the mid-nineteenth-century Midwest. At the same time, however, this would be a newer pietism, influenced by the American soil in which it was planted. Nearly a century ago, more than one hundred and fifty pastors had migrated to Missouri from the German mission houses. Poorly educated, they were unprepared to confront the religious freethinking migrants.

Ordinarily in Germany, the pathway to church ministry required a university degree, an option only for the elite. Consequently, peasants and farmers were excluded from formal congregational ministry. The mission societies, however, welcomed any man regardless of background and social status—peasants, farmers, craftsmen, tradesmen, teachers, and others. While their training was not in the academic programs of the universities, they enrolled in introductory classes, Bible and theological study, and pastoral and mission courses. Their education was practically oriented, with the focus on sufficient training to operate in the mission field.

As these missionaries entered Missouri, they began to function as pastors of rapidly growing congregations made up of an ever-increasing number of immigrants with large families that filled the pews. It was both a baby boom and a religious boom, and the need for faith formation was clear. With churches now established and pastors in place to serve them, the next challenge was how to raise up leaders from among the new immigrants themselves. The supply from Europe was undoubtedly a short-term solution.

PREDICTING PROPHETS

Social scientists have an excellent record of producing theories but an abysmal record of successfully predicting specific social phenomena with those same theories. French sociologist Émile Durkheim created convincing theories about how social integration and alienation are related to whether one commits suicide. His theories make intuitive sense—even common sense—some might say. When Durkheim conducted the first quantitative analysis in sociology, it was clear that predicting who would voluntarily end their lives was hardly going to be an exact science.[2]

Answers to the question of where prophets come from are at least as challenging to predict as who commits suicide and who doesn't. To make matters more complicated, anyone who addresses the question of why a prophet arises then and not now or why her and not him must include the unpredictable X-factor of God—the One who calls the prophet when, where, and who God chooses. Why Jeremiah, who was only a child? Why Elijah, who killed pagan prophets but ran from a queen? Why Samuel, who thought he knew best who would be king? Or why Walter Brueggemann from Blackburn, Missouri, who would write far more scrolls than his Old Testament peers, but at age eighty-nine, when approached about the writing of his biography, responded with "Nothing very interesting has happened in my life?" And who still muses over whether he has contributed anything of importance in his life. How was it that Brueggemann, growing up poor as a pastor's kid in Blackburn, Missouri, would be called by the Almighty to embrace and advocate for a new way of reading Scripture and help to salvage biblical interpretation from the moribund path that it was on—a path that had little to offer the church and its pastors in the later twentieth century?

As if anticipating this question by the fortieth anniversary of *The Prophetic Imagination*'s initial publication in 1978, Brueggemann writes that "Evidently, God can 'raise up prophets' and authorize prophetic voices and deeds in the fullness of God's own freedom, anywhere, anytime, in any circumstance. If however, we are to think from the human side of the matter, it will not surprise that some social environments are more hospitable than others to prophets and more likely to be the locus of their emergence."[3]

Like any good prophet and social scientist, Brueggemann's lifelong work has reflected both God's freedom to act with agency and the usefulness—albeit limited—of the social sciences to explain human behavior. In other words, while he believes that God is free to raise up prophets anywhere and at any time, Brueggemann also recognizes that the calling of prophets occurs within particular social and cultural contexts. In this way, it may be possible to get a glimpse of why and what God is up to when calling prophets.

Brueggemann suggests several criteria that are necessary ingredients for the appearance of prophets, including belonging to communities that are in tension with the dominant community, corporate memory that connects one generation after another to the past, recognizing and articulating corporate pain, offering hope, and speaking a language across the generations that only those inside can recognize. In sum, tension, a known past, pain, hope, and an ongoing conversation across generations are the objective landmarks of the habitat from which prophets come. And to this must be added a sense of marginalization and identification with the marginalized.

If Walter's life were a sociological model, wherein one is trying to identify the variables or factors that most predict his life and work, like most sociological modeling, adequate explanations, and precise predictions are elusive. Still, some clarity comes into view the longer one listens to Walter and those who know him well. His knowledge and a high view of the biblical text, his love for the God of that text, the value he places on community, his recognition that the church alone is the carrier of the Story, his formation in the Evangelical Synod of North America, his respect for and closeness to his pastor-father, and his commitment to the dialogical are among some of the ingredients most critical to producing Walter Brueggemann. But after all is said and done, much about Walter's story remains a mystery. When the Apostle Paul observed the dark glass through which we see most anything and anyone, he knew of what he spoke.

HABITUS

Besides the habitat or geography of prophets, it is helpful to consider French sociologist Pierre Bourdieu, who moves beyond habitat to "habitus," by which he means not only the objective realities of one's landscape but how these realities sneak into the subconscious rear of the brain and become the taken-for-granted realities of the worlds in which one resides.[4] Habitus is about the internalization of the objective realities, and internalization is the process by which the landscape "out there" becomes the landscape within oneself. Habitus is that part of the religious world that lights up one's soul, that connects with the personal experience and fire of the divine already within oneself, where the rituals of communion and baptism move beyond the objective activity to feed one's spiritual hunger, and where the truths of God's words are experienced as truth in one's being. While the habitat may be the same for a group of people, the degree to which one absorbs or resonates with the habitus varies mysteriously from individual to individual. Growing up in the same habitat, one rejects the faith, and another becomes an evangelist, one becomes a pagan and one a preacher, and one a prophet and another a party animal. Prophets in particular absorb and internalize and accept as true the religion of their landscape.

Reflecting late in life on the differences between the two brothers who grew up in the same habitat and habitus, Edward, the oldest and the least willing to conform to the expectations of the world in which he and Walter grew up, introduced Walter in a series of lectures this way:

> In the third grade in Salem, MO, your teacher conferred with our parents because they could not keep you busy, and my teacher conferred with them because she thought I was a little slow. . . . I showed you how to get. . . . to Elmhurst College where you distinguished yourself in studies, and I played basketball. . . . You went to class. I cut class. . . . We entered Eden Seminary. . . . You visited the library. I visited the College of Nursing. . . . I dug in the garden, you dug for the Dead Sea Scrolls. . . . I spent these last fifty or so years an ecclesiastical mechanic . . . while you dedicated to diligent study that has helped all of us . . . overhaul our understanding of the meaning of scripture.[5]

The difference between Ed and Walter illustrates that while habitat matters, it is a poor predictor of who becomes the prophet. Habitus helps more perhaps, as long as it is not used deterministically and recognizes the vast variance between individuals. And finally, none of this matters if the call of the Almighty and the prophet's obedience are absent.

The habitat in which Walter grew up was particularly conducive to a prophet's emergence. He had a profound sensitivity and personal response to the holy. He experienced a divine call to a prophetic vocation. And he obediently responded to that call. Still, knowing what has formed and informed him, the man remains a mystery, as are all formed with the divine imprint upon them. Sometimes in Brueggemann's case, the veil lifts enough to suggest one answer, and then he pivots again. Sometimes his point is clear until he offers a counterpoint. Just when one feels oriented by words of comfort and hope, Brueggemann suddenly thrusts his audience into disorientation, and hearts are filled with doubt and fear. But then the clouds lift and what appears to be a new space is still the old one, but with one having a new orientation.

As a biographical subject, Brueggemann defies reductionist portraits of himself, just as he denies reductionism of the biblical text and the God of that text. For one who embraces typologies that have served his interpretive work so effectively, he also recognizes that typologies, or "ideal types" in the words of sociologist Max Weber, are imperfect.[6] Walter is grounded deeply in the reality that worlds we have made and continue to make are messy, perhaps because he also sees the God who oversees those worlds as a bit ambiguous, in recovery, and an unsettled spirit. A God who cannot be fully measured, a God who pivots just when we imagined we knew where he was going, and a God whose mystery and preference for openness and unpredictability are enough to keep us on our toes.

WALTER'S PARENTS

Walter was the youngest of three sons, his older brother Charles having died as a one-year-old before Walter's birth. Walter's mother would never be the same following her son's death. She remains in the background of Walter's memories of childhood—overly protective, quiet, and anxious. She was at the same time an energetic, caring, good-humored mother who made the life of the family work with general happiness and wellbeing. It was his pastor-father August whom Walter would seek to emulate, and from whom he has never been far removed.

Walter's father was the next-youngest son of Frederick Wilhelm and Augusta (Bueker) Brueggemann. Frederick migrated from the Hannover region of Prussia as a fourteen-year-old in 1857, while Augusta was born in Missouri in 1854. Her parents, like Frederick, had migrated from Prussia, specifically from Lippe-Depmot. Her parents' origins were deep in the heart of the Prussian Union, a religious partnership between two Reformation Protestant traditions.

Of all the communities in which August Brueggemann pastored, Burnside, Missouri, is the one Walter most remembers as his home. It was a small community of three hundred people and four churches— St. Paul's Evangelical and Reformed Church, the local Missouri Synod congregation, a Methodist congregation, and the Black church that was invisible to the 270 white folks in town. For Walter, the church was the main matrix of his life, with the entire family invested in the congregation. While his home life was a warm, embracing environment, his mother was always nervous that the Brueggemann boys would do something to embarrass their father. Though their family was relatively poor, that thought never dawned on Walter at the time. A rural pastor was poorly paid but they always had enough for everything, and August and Hilda were shrewd with what they did have.

Besides the isolation, Walter soon became aware of the inferior nature of his father's education as well as that provided by his high school. There was much to be humble about in his growing up. To strengthen his boys' educational experience, August asked the local school board to offer Latin to his sons. This was not a regularly offered elective and so the beloved teacher Esther Yowell, who knew Latin, was invited to teach the Brueggemann boys. But illness prevented Yowell from continuing, and the school administration then called upon the one other member of the community who knew Latin—the pastor of the local Missouri Synod Lutheran Church. But, as mentioned earlier, there was a history between Walter's father August and the reverend. Upon his arrival to Blackburn as the new Missouri Synod pastor, August paid a visit to the new pastor to welcome him, but the pastor refused to stand in greeting or acknowledge August's presence, and so August turned around and left the stoic Lutheran in his chair. The old quarrels from the German homeland continued to manifest themselves between those who had embraced the Prussian Union and those who had rejected it. But both groups ended up migrating to Missouri together and living side by side. And the difference between the two remained evident more than a century later and thousands of miles from where the schism began.

THE FRAGILITY OF LIFE

Walter grew up experiencing empathy for those on the margins of his community. He had a deep sense of the toughness of life for people in a rural community, who were "willy-nilly" dependent upon the providential care of God. It had to rain—everything depended on that, and this created a certain unspoken valuing of life. Farmers had great respect for the growing season, the impact of weather, and the fact that they were dependent on what was dealt to them season by season. Walter found this to be an early lesson in the dangers of self-sufficiency. This habitat also gave Walter a strong work ethic and a deep moral grounding in a world in which you were as good as your word. His rural childhood also produced an impetus to study because he knew he did not want to plow, bale hay, and change tires in zero degrees at the local service station for the rest of his life. He modestly resented having to do that work, finding it neither satisfying nor ever knowing quite what he was doing nor if he had done it right. He learned that farmers either assume that everyone knows how to do what needs to be done or will figure it out.

Walter grew up with some resentment toward the church that kept his father poor when its members had resources with which they could have paid him more. Walter's attentiveness to those in poverty in his later work was profoundly personal and grew out of the pain he felt from the economic injustices experienced by his father. In Walter's teenage mind, his father's poverty was not necessary but was due to the parsimoniousness and grudging behavior of the people August served. They gave August his marching orders and he slowly fought back, but Walter felt deeply inferior and disadvantaged, and something about that inferiority was under his skin.

He would always remain in touch with that insecurity and his father's pain.

The loss of their first child forever marked Hilda Brueggemann with anxiety and concern about the safety of her two other sons. Walter experienced his mother as overly protective to the point of being oppressive. After bathing, she required the boys to place their wet heads inside a warm oven, so they wouldn't get sick. They needed to avoid doing anything that might bring shame on their family and the way to do that was "right living." Hilda sensed the precariousness of life as well as the risks that the church imposed on her. Walter's mother actively participated in church doings, teaching church school, leading music (vocal, organ, and piano), and in the Dorcas Society. Still, she often stayed at home, experiencing the aloneness that came with being a pastor's wife. The share she had in her mother's estate was a disappointment to her, and while her four brothers prospered in Kansas, she was left mostly with hard work. She nevertheless brought great energy and spirit to her work in and for the family.

Hilda had a critical role to play in the local congregation of Blackburn. She served as organist and pianist for her husband. He counted on her to select the hymns each week. But Hilda was chronically anxious about the possibility August might preach something that aggravated the members. The pastor had little protection within the congregation, being accountable to a Church Council of three stern older men who played the most prominent leadership role and carried the governing authority of a congregation. The major families in the church rotated leadership positions and kept a close check on the work of the family.

On Sunday afternoons, following the church service, Walter's mother stood inside the parsonage, peering through the window at the Council members who gathered at the front of the church each Sunday following the service to discuss the business of the church. She always assumed that they were talking about August, who faced a lot of criticism in the congregation. Of particular note was the debate in the 1940s over whether to cease or continue preaching in German. Walter's father insisted on the transition to English, against the will of some. A compromise was made whereby German was preached once a month. Walter's father was convinced that if the church wanted to retain its youth, this transition to English was necessary.

Things were also more challenging for August because his educational attainment was relatively weak. He completed his high school education and entered farming as a career, but a local physician in their town of Bland consistently pressed August to consider the ministry. The young men of the Evangelical Synod undoubtedly faced pressure as the older generation looked with anxiety to a future for leaders from Missouri who could mediate the Union tradition in a new land. When August responded to the call to ministry he was already older than most other candidates. The pathway forward was to enroll at Eden Seminary in Webster Groves, just east of St. Louis. This seminary had been patterned somewhat after the mission house training programs in Germany that had prepared missionaries to establish churches in Missouri. Those training programs accepted anyone regardless of trade, and taught introductory education courses, theology, pastoral, and mission courses. So from the beginning, the Missouri congregations were accustomed to leaders with relatively low levels of education and training—unlike their Lutheran and Reformed churches of the Northeast, which had higher educational expectations of their clergy. Had the Evangelical Synod expected the same, few congregations would have been established in the New Rhineland.

Early in his ministry he and Hilda had experienced great success at their assignment in Tilden, Nebraska, at the height of the Great Depression between 1931 and 1935 (Walter was born in 1933). While pastors were seen as important to the functioning of the church, the governance, structure, and social organization belonged to the congregation. In fact, in Blackburn's St. Paul's congregation, August had to request permission from the Church Council for any expense over twenty-five dollars.

Though pastors were often marginal to the congregation's life, congregations took pride in acknowledging the pastors who emerged from their spiritual wombs. August and his younger brother Albert are identified as such in their family's home congregation at Bland, Missouri. So it was a very significant occasion when, on June 29, 1958, back in St. Paul's church in Blackburn, where August had faced so much difficulty and so much challenge, that he would be able to ordain both of his living sons—Edward and Walter. The church was filled.

CALLED

Two significant spiritual experiences shaped Walter within his German pietist tradition. At thirteen, youth were expected to attend two years of confirmation instruction every Saturday morning. For Walter and Ed, August was the teacher. More than anyone else, it would be August who formed the spiritual context within which Walter grew up and who offered his son the most significant spiritual formation of his early years. For two years August was Walter's confirmation teacher. They bonded to one another. Walter memorized the entire Evangelical catechism. Candidates were tested on their knowledge of the catechism in front of the congregation, though the test was often generous. Less demand was placed on his brother Ed, but he too passed with flying colors.

At confirmation, it was the tradition that the pastor picked out a Scripture text that would be a confirmation verse particularly appropriate to the candidate. For older people, the confirmation verse was often the one used at their funeral. Walter's dad picked out Psalm 119:105: "Thy word is a lamp unto my feet and a light unto my path." Clearly, given his life, August got it just right. "Yes, Scripture is everything in my life; yes, yes, yes," says Walter. Indeed, given what his son has achieved, perhaps August was every bit the prophetic voice that his son would become—a son who repeatedly named and invoked the gifts and callings that he would see in others just as his father August did with him.

Every summer of his high school years, Walter attended the Synod's youth summer camp led by young pastors. These camp experiences were a lot of fun, and he thought the pastors who led were the "neatest people." The camp was a prominent part of his decision to pursue ministry. August was a mentor to many of the young pastors, so the experience of a "thick" community continued to reinforce Walter's call. The summer camps emphasized church vocation in a way that readied Walter to hear and answer the invitation to ministry. Participants regularly went through the wonder at the Friday night consecration service, and those liturgical moments were important for Walter. The camps had three classes every day for a week, something in Bible, the arts, and so on. Singing and folk dancing and group-building activities informed and strengthened identity and community. Walter experienced camp as a good place where the whole conversation was about discipleship. Bonfires and lots of prayers for practically committing their lives were highlights. One of the gimmicks used on the last day was writing a letter to oneself about the week's experience. Then six months later, a camp counselor would send the letter. It was a marvelous way of keeping that experience available to the participants. These were very important religious and cultural markers for Walter's experience of church and his future call.

One of the practices among German farmers was bringing in their produce in the fall—the act of "bringing in the sheaves." The church hosted an annual mission festival where they invited guests—usually a missionary—to preach in the morning and the afternoon. The recurring pattern of these festivals influenced Walter's awareness of the essential missional dimension of the church. One speaker in particular, O. Walter Wagner, was a progressive ahead of his time. He spent hours talking to Walter and Ed about ministry. He was raising money for the relief of war-torn Europe. While that was the "gig" he was on, he really talked to the boys about the underlying claims of the Gospel. These were very influential conversations for Walter's ongoing discernment of his call while still in high school. Walter's high school Sunday School teacher, Walter Borchers, also showed genuine interest in the boys in his class, remaining with them for four years. A farmer, he never prepared anything, but came every Sunday well-informed and created a safe space to talk, banter, and laugh with the boys.

Walter's decision to follow his father into ministry was reasonably straightforward. He assumed he would go through college and seminary and do what his dad did. He had great admiration for his father. Walter's horizon was fairly small, and he did not understand much about the great issues of the world yet, but he could see that the way his father was spending his life was important. Walter wanted to do the same. At the end of World War II in 1945, St. Paul's church placed stars at the front of the sanctuary for all those in the service and the service included recognition of the one Gold Star member who died in combat. Walter remembers the special liturgy his father oversaw for taking those stars down and returning them to the families during the ritual. This was a very defining moment for a twelve-year-old in "seeing my dad's" work as a pastor.

CATECHISM

The subculture of Blackburn, Missouri, and the many other German communities settled by the descendants of the 1817 Prussian Union, was composed of minority enclaves with thick social connections. At the level of ethnicity, Walter's community was out of sync with broader American society, but as a pastor's child in the ministry subculture within an ethnic subculture he was doubly marginalized. Added to that was his awareness of his family's poverty and isolation and such situations can result in deep insecurity, a lack of networks from which to discover mentors, and anxiety about always being behind.

Walter was the product of a religious tradition that, in its simplicity and pietism, was out of touch with the dominant American Protestantism that engaged culture and embraced it. He was raised on the catechism which is a mix of Luther and Calvin. The last question of the catechism he has forgotten, but the answer he has not: "Lord Jesus, for thee I live, for thee, I suffer, I die! Lord Jesus, thine will I be in life and death! Grant me, O Lord, eternal salvation. Amen."[7] The Synod's catechism was simple, and mostly just Scripture. He memorized all of it at thirteen years of age, but he had no idea what it was talking about. Still, it represents the immediacy of faith that belongs to the German pietism he grew up with, a pietism that reacted against the "acres and acres of scholastic theology" of Lutheranism. Pietism's response to such Scholasticism was "none of that really helps us at all." Exactly what Walter said for years about historical criticism!

The thinness of interpretation in the catechism was intentional and reflected the pietism of the tradition from which the Synod had emerged, a pietism that emphasized commitment to Christ and a life of obedient discipleship. The lack of interpretive work within the catechism also reflected the "irenic" nature of the Prussian Union and its Missouri descendants. They gave broad latitude to theological differences and embraced an ecumenical spirit. "In essentials unity, in non-essentials liberty, and in all things charity" was their motto.[8] If one is interested in unity around the Scriptures, perhaps the less said the better. The catechism reflected the Synod leaders' high view of Scripture. They were traditionalists who took the Scripture seriously but not literally. The impact of the catechism meant that Walter has a history of following the Bible. But what was the pathway that the Missouri descendants of the Prussian Union took to ensure that children of that Union, like Walter, would be shaped so powerfully by its values a century later?

RELIGIOUS COMMUNITIES

German congregations flourished under the guidance and leadership of the German mission-house pastors. As they did so, some of these leaders began to ask about the kind of organization or structure best suited for these descendants of the Prussian Union. The congregations were clearly in a different religious context from that of the "fatherland." America was a religious free market as compared to the state church environment of Germany and Switzerland, and, clearly, church involvement in the New World would be based upon voluntarism rather than coercion. Churches would survive and thrive based on their competitive edge rather than because they received state support. How best to organize an enduring church in this new space?

Six leaders who came to Missouri from the mission houses in Germany and Switzerland met together in October 1840 to address, at least in part, such questions. The outcome of that meeting was their decision to create the Kirchenverein des Westens or the German Evangelical Church Society of the West. The society's founders intended to remain spiritually connected to the Evangelical Union Church of their homeland. The mission houses, however, were free of any formal connection to the Union's church government in Germany, and so there were also no formal ties of the new society congregations of Missouri to the church from which they had sprung.

Given the American context, however, it was inevitable that within a generation the close organic connection to Germany would begin to thin. Leaders began to call for the kinds of structure and tools common among state churches in Germany—a standard hymnal, catechism, and faith statement. They recognized the value of these in sustaining and passing on the faith, of nurturing the religious culture and sentiment from which they had come. And with members coming from various state churches, what would hold them together now? Work was initiated on a catechism for their new context and completed in 1847. It was translated into English in 1890, and then it was revised around 1927.

Foundational to this catechism is the statement that captures the ecumenical, pietistic, and irenic nature of this early church:

> We recognize the Evangelical Church as that communion which acknowledges the Holy scriptures of the Old and New Testament as the Word of God as the sole and infallible rule of faith and life, and accepts the interpretation of the Holy scriptures as given in the symbolic books of the Lutheran and the Reformed Church, the most important being: the Augsburg Confession, Luther's and the Heidelberg Catechisms, In so far as they agree; but where they disagree, we adhere strictly to the passages of Holy scripture bearing on the subject, and avail ourselves of the liberty of conscience prevailing in the Evangelical Church.[9]

The printing of denominational materials was often done at Eden Publishing House in St. Louis. Walter and his family often visited the publishing house, and Walter was in awe of the steadfast seriousness of the work of publishing for the church.

Looking back a century later, pastor and church historian Frederick Trost describes the Synod catechism as presenting

a faith worthy of emulation—not faith easily tossed aside . . . but faith anchored in
the fertile ground of deep, joyous, hopeful
conviction. . . . [The] German-speaking
immigrants of nearly two hundred years ago
understood who they were. They perceived
themselves more as a Liebesgemeinschaft
(a community of love) than as a Lehrgemein-
schaft (a community of doctrine).[10]

The revised catechism of 1927 brought changes
that reflected the ongoing assimilation of the Evangelical Synod into the larger American Protestant scene,
in some ways diluting the origins of the Synod's early
Prussian Union rootage, a process that would continue
through organizational mergers with other denominational bodies. The character of the German Lutheran
tradition was weakened in the Revised Edition of the
Evangelical Catechism, and there were more nods to
the Reformed tradition. This revised catechism of 1927
would be the one that Walter Brueggemann studied
and memorized as a teenager, and the twin streams of
Reformed and Lutheran are reflected in his work, perhaps in part due to the revised catechism. The question whether Walter Brueggemann leans more toward
Luther or Calvin remains an ongoing debate. Even
Walter, who resists being pigeonholed and reduced to
categories, does not offer complete clarity as to how he
sees himself.

NEW NAME AND MERGER

In 1870, a different group of leaders met to address the
continued organizational needs of their pastors and

congregations, renaming themselves the "Evangelical Synod of North America." The language change reflected the pressures of assimilation that these leaders were experiencing by living in the United States where all religious groups face the pressures of Americanization—to conform to the organizational structures of a nation birthed out of Enlightenment rationality and its emphasis on individual freedom and expression.

Still, these leaders considered themselves not as a "Church" but as a "Synod" related to the Evangelical Church of the Old Prussian Union. They had pietistic roots and a commitment to being an irenic community of faith where the focus was on loving God and neighbor. "Love of neighbor" in the Evangelical Synod of North America included the establishment of orphanages and other diaconic works such as hospitals. Unlike the German Lutherans and those of the Reformed tradition who had entered the United States a century or two prior, pastors such as August Brueggemann were still relatively close to their ethnic and religious roots in the fatherland. There had been little time for translation in the American context, particularly because the first generation of pastors were themselves imports from the German mission houses of Basel, Bremen, and Barmen.

In some ways, pastors in August's generation were among the first generation of Evangelical Synod pastors in the German churches, and thus faced the challenges of any first-generation immigrant. But for these pastors, the challenges were not only personal in terms of how they adjusted to the New World: What would they retain from the Old World? What would they cast off? What would they renovate? The challenges were also theological, spiritual, and ecclesial. How was a pastor to pass on the beliefs of the tradition to people now being influenced by Roman Catholicism, the Lutheran

Missouri Synod churches, and the new personal freedom and opportunity offered in these new lands? How
should congregations arrange and structure themselves
to best socialize their children in the Union tradition,
children being drawn to many alternatives and growing up in a context so very different from most of their
parents?

For among the descendants of the Prussian Union,
the Gospel was a relatively simple affair: "Love God
and neighbor" and remember "In essentials unity, in
non-essentials liberty, and in all things charity." Such
simplicity excluded the need for extensive education
and learning, and of course, this was consistent with
the origins of German pietism against the high Scholasticism and rationality of the Enlightenment-influenced
Lutherans of Germany. At this point, as well, the pull
to assimilate with the northeastern Protestant churches
was only beginning to be felt. Down the road, the
Synod would merge with the Reformed Church in
Pennsylvania to become the Evangelical and Reformed
Church from 1934 to 1957. This group would then join
the Congregational Church to form the UCC. So while
Walter was growing up in Blackburn there was much
dynamism in the air and the winds of change were less
intense than they would become for pastors and congregations in coming decades. There was still a lot of
the German homeland being breathed in the habitat
around Blackburn.

ROOTS

Among those who know Walter Brueggemann well,
including those who wrote, studied, and taught with
him, few can articulate precisely what Walter meant

by his lifelong identification with German Evangelical Pietism. This is no surprise, perhaps, given the ambiguous use of "evangelical" in the New World that awaited the children of the Prussian Union who migrated by the tens of thousands to Missouri between 1840 and 1890.

Nor should it be a surprise that the term "pietism" in the United States has been little understood and largely disappeared as a religious identity. Pietism's call for a "heart religion" and personal faith and life with God, over against the Scholasticism of Lutheranism, faced difficulty in translation in the New World. The pressures to assimilate with American Protestant denominational forms resulted in a lost memory of both the term "pietism" and its embodied qualities. But it is indeed this rootedness in German Evangelical Pietism, with its characteristics of ecumenism (union), life with God (pietism), and a simple commitment to love God and neighbor (irenic) that are responsible for the exceptional body of work that Walter Brueggemann has produced in the past six decades.

In Walter's words, German Evangelical Pietism reflected a "peaceable" posture of "wanting to get along with each other, not prone to pick a fight. It did not fuss with theological matters. The tradition was a kind of a give people room and let people get along and love Jesus. Can we care for poor, sick, and vulnerable people and just get on with it? Early on the Synod initiated institutions of care for orphans and disabled persons. So it is very simple!" German evangelical pietism reflects the qualities of the prophetic imagination described by Brueggemann in his hideaway office and that would erupt so surprisingly a few years later. The habitat and habitus into which Brueggemann was dropped at birth had all the makings of "an alternative reality" to the religious quarrels of Europe and the many that have continued in the New World.

Brueggemann's voice reminded the church of that alternative reality amid a nation torn by conflict in the mid-to-late twentieth century. By the time he did so the qualities of German evangelical pietism were already subjugated to the commitments of a church absorbed with addressing the world's problems but forgetting that answers were as close as the biblical text and the God of that text. While many heard Brueggemann's call to arms on behalf of the marginalized, many missed his point that the call emerged from a living text containing a living God with answers for a living people. "I am grateful," says Brueggemann, "that the progressives were my habitat, but these same progressives often missed seeing the full scope of the prophetic imagination." When pressed as to why the reiteration of a prophetic imagination must be repeated again and again across generations, Walter responds: "Because the church just keeps becoming domesticated to the dominant culture."

Pietism has always faced difficulty within the rational, modern societies within which it emerges and against which it reacts. Writing a century ago, Evangelical Synod of North America pastor Hugo Kamphausen noted:

> Pietism has never found a healthy easy-going relationship to the world, the culture, and its economy. It has not been able to set up system of social teaching that might help to shape our political and social life according to a Christian pattern. In this area, others have taken the lead and it will take a bit of doing for pietism to relate to these larger areas of our social life and make its influence felt.[11]

While Troeltsch had earlier argued that pietism's close identity with Jesus's teaching made it more likely to survive in sectarian forms of religious expression than in church or denominational forms, Kamphausen disagrees and remained optimistic that church and denominational forms could be carriers of a lively pietism that emphasized word and deed as well as heart and head.

Time would tell whether Troeltsch or Kamphausen was right regarding the North American Evangelical Synod and the pressures it would face in the New World. Walter Brueggemann himself aligns with Troeltsch's prediction, noting that the UCC, of which the Evangelical Synod was a founding body, has largely failed to integrate or acknowledge the seed of pietism in any meaningful way. And perhaps this is why a prophet who remembered the ancient ideals was called by God to remind a compromised and coopted church of "an alternative reality to the one that lies in front of us!" And seeing that alternative takes a bit of prophetic imagination. But once articulated in 1978, Brueggemann would spend the rest of his days sharing that imagination just about everywhere and with anyone who will listen!

PART TWO

THREE

Imagination Everywhere

Every text has an ax to grind.

Walter Brueggemann

Brueggemann awoke earlier than usual, ahead of the alarm clock he set the night before. He had slept fitfully, lying awake wondering why and how he had followed his calling this far. He thought for a moment of his father August, and how proud he would be of his youngest son, whose efforts to go against the scholarly flow of biblical studies had led to this moment on November 17, 1990. "I've indeed been ahead of the pack," Brueggemann thought to himself. The truth was that he had always worked as if from behind the pack! But his efforts to dismantle the historical-critical analysis of the biblical text and move toward rhetorical analysis with a social scientific interpretive bent had contributed to today's legitimation of both himself as a scholar but also his mode of analysis.

Later that evening, Brueggemann would give the presidential address to the Society of Biblical Literature, the oldest and most prestigious of the scholarly societies that focused on interdisciplinary research about the Bible. August, his father with no high school diploma, had struggled to get through Eden Seminary. His son had written twenty books since the eruption of *The Prophetic Imagination* in 1978. Brueggemann also transferred in 1986 from his beloved Eden Seminary to the more prestigious and financially better endowed Columbia Seminary in Atlanta, Georgia. Offered a lighter teaching load, a full-time secretary, and greater financial support for his research and writing, Brueggemann had taken the bait—though tension with the direction of Eden Seminary under new presidential leadership and the transition of Brueggemann out as Dean of Academic Affairs had made the bait more alluring this time.

It was certainly not the first offer he had received since the publication of *The Prophetic Imagination*, but it was the first he accepted. Leaving Eden Seminary behind, a seminary that in fifteen years he had formed in his own image in many ways, was more difficult than he had anticipated. And his departure was hard on his colleagues also, many of whom he was responsible for hiring. Leaving idyllic Webster Groves where his boys had grown up within walking distance of the seminary, boys he whistled at to get their ball gloves for a round of pitch and catch following another long day at work, pulled at his heart also. Both had grown up so quickly and both had become so responsible. Both worked like their father, too hard he sometimes thought. But a look in the mirror reminded him of the reasons they did so. And they didn't hesitate to remind him also when he dared bring it up.

Little did he know, however, that his future colleagues were nearly giddy with disbelief at their luck in landing a colleague of Brueggemann's stature. And while some of their children had no idea who their parents were so excited about, rumors had begun to circulate among their daughters that the Brueggemann package included sons Jim and John. Brueggemann was not simply a rising star, but a star already in Old Testament studies. He also reflected the character of Columbia Seminary at the time, with its strong focus on preparing persons for ministry. So it was a great thing for those waiting in Atlanta.

Shifting his thoughts back to the upcoming evening, Brueggemann reflected again on the eruption of *The Prophetic Imagination* more than a decade ago and how its bestseller status had moved him from relative obscurity to become among the most recognizable name of any American theologian of the day! And with so much of the positive response coming from pastors and the church, he also realized that the very reason some of his peers had neglected to acknowledge the value of his work—because it was a scholarship for the church—was also the reason for the book's success. There were few other scholars at the SBL meeting that year who had come even close to the number of books Brueggemann had sold, let alone just for one title. If the ax he had been called to grind was *The Prophetic Imagination*, Brueggemann had been grinding if for all it was worth and he was not about to stop on this momentous day! It remained the primary lens through which he interpreted the biblical text. In many ways, this had always been and always would be true.

A DREAM FULFILLED

During his years of relatively little writing when weighed down by dean of the faculty responsibilities, Brueggemann had dreamed of today. He had been recognized over the past year for the scholarly contributions he had made to biblical studies in building upon the work of his beloved teacher from Union Seminary, who had brought the presidential address to the SBL in 1968. Dr. James Muilenburg was now deceased, but his major contribution in shifting the field from historical criticism to rhetorical analysis had been a monumental achievement. He had used his 1968 presidential address to lay out his radical redirection of biblical studies.[1] Not a strong scholar, the address was one of the best articulations of his approach to writing and remains so today.[2]

Brueggemann would be sure to laud Muilenburg's influence in his lecture that evening. He had felt so proud back in 1968 to be identified as one of Muilenburg's leading students along with Phyllis Trible and Norman Gottwald. And though the other two of Muilenburg's students would eventually be named to the presidential post of the SBL, Brueggemann felt some small bit of satisfaction in getting there ahead of them. He remembers wondering back in 1968 whether being buried at a small seminary like Eden, Brueggemann would ever hear his name called to the SBL lectern to give the presidential address that Muilenburg was on the verge of offering. But even as he listened to his beloved teacher that night, he realized that a decade since sitting in Muilenburg's classroom, and despite the burden of being dean, Brueggemann had moved beyond his mentor in several key theoretical areas. These were all part of the stirring and whirling within and around Brueggemann that would lead to the 1978 eruption of *The Prophetic Imagination* and today's lecture.

A SINGLE MENTOR

Brueggemann's mind also drifted to his friend and mentor, Bernard Anderson, who retired from Princeton

Seminary, who like Brueggemann had always felt a bit like an outsider. Upon Anderson's retirement, Brueggemann was offered Anderson's academic position but declined. Though turning down the post, the process of interviewing had brought the two together, and Brueggemann recognized that Anderson had begun to pay attention to his work. Anderson served on the SBL presidential nominating committee when Brueggemann's name was put forward as a candidate. Brueggemann only later realized that getting nominated was not as complicated as he had thought since one only needed "two friends" on the nominating committee.

But Walter also learned from Anderson how to not worry about the big picture of stigma and academic competition and focus on the text in front of him. He saw Anderson do remarkable things with the text. He also saw in Anderson a willingness to forge ahead with his work without worrying about what other people thought about it, or whether it was going to be well received. And that contributed to needed courage for Walter. He knew that both pastors and prophets were in dire need of courage, and recognized that he could now be a model of that for them.

Before Anderson, Brueggemann had many excellent teachers at Elmhurst College, Eden Seminary, and Union Seminary, and had worked side by side with a "Who's Who" list of Old and New Testament colleagues. Yet he never considered any of these individuals to be mentors. The only other person he calls a mentor was his father August. Blackburn, MO was not particularly oriented toward offering mentors to its youth. Brueggemann had learned the hard way to figure things out on his own as a teenager in Blackburn, MO. The farmers and service station mechanic he worked for never bothered to mentor him. Mentoring was not a known commodity in a town where "hard knocks" was the primary teacher. Brueggemann never knew whether he had gotten it right or not—success was measured by whether the hay stayed where it belonged in the loft and whether a customer lost their tires or not while driving down the road.

ON THE EDGE OF THE ACADEMY

Learning to do things on his own, and assuming that is how one got ahead, had generally served Brueggemann well. In course after course, he would eventually rise to the top. This approach was sufficient for learning. This "lone ranger" character trait, combined with Brueggemann's near-photographic recall, blue-collar work ethic, and unusual curiosity to know the "other," set him apart from the academic herd. He wasted no time on frivolities—it was all work for Brueggemann. But Brueggemann's humble beginnings and his tenure in a small seminary meant that he always felt like an outsider among the giants of the field from Harvard, Yale, and Princeton, among others. He felt inferior because of his midwestern roots in rural Missouri, his lack of knowledge and fluency in German and the languages of the antiquities, and his decision to primarily publish his work for pastors and church audiences.

This meant that his work, written for church practitioners and not scholars, sometimes failed to include the jargonese, nuancing, and denseness that validated high achievement in academia. These were all intentional decisions on his part—to always teach at seminaries, to train pastors, and to serve the church over the academy. His elevation to SBL president did much to legitimize his scholarly work, at least to himself. And twelve years since *The Prophetic Imagination,* perhaps only Brueggemann needed the reminder of just how far he had come and how good his work was. By now, Brueggemann's "imagination" could be heard just about everywhere in the halls and ballrooms and book sales tables of the New Orleans Marriott that November.

In actuality, his internal resentment had already been receding before 1990. Brueggemann had managed to get over his "Harvey Cox days" when he imagined that he would one day be "a hot shot scholar." Somewhere along the way, he discovered that the church was the natural habitat for his work, a discovery that brought him greater freedom but only increased the tense relationship with the guild and the big players in Old Testament studies who did not think Brueggemann was a real scholar. The old guard looked askance at younger scholars who were not so inured to historical criticism. While it took time, Brueggemann got over his "disease" of historical criticism by finally accepting that he could be a different kind of scholar whose scholarship was a ministry to the church. Again he remembered his father August's commitment to the church despite injustice, disrespect, and abuse from those he served.

Brueggemann found satisfaction on this important day in remembering that he had never moved far from his father or the German evangelical pietism mediated to him by August, a pietism that had little time for quarrels and church disputes in its quest to "love God and neighbor." And despite the sense of alienation and marginalization that Brueggemann experienced, he had little interest in arguing about his impact or justifying his scholarly existence to his detractors. Doing so only took away from his precious writing time. Undoubtedly his knack for working and keeping his hand to the plow was in part responsible for his prolific productivity—and that posture of moving forward without looking back was honed in Blackburn, MO, where any farmer with any sense at all knows that turning around to see how straight one's corn rows are only ruins what lies ahead. Letters in response to those who opposed his work for theological or scholarly reasons always received a written response, direct and to the point but always generous and courteous.

The ecumenical, irenic, and pietistic (not pious) posture of his ancestors also had made Brueggemann an impatient player in the niceties of guild norms and debates. If his habitat was the church and he had something the church needed, he had no time for debates on the ins and outs of particular theological ideas and intricacies that created closed categories and that siphoned off all the embarrassment of the text the way that historical criticism had done so. For it was the embarrassment that gave the text the juice! This irascibility also manifested itself in an unwillingness to debate the certainties he held to—he was known to walk away from such conversations with a response of "that sounds about right," allowing both parties to save face.

Historical criticism flattened and deadened the text, reflecting the very field about which he had long felt so much ambivalence—desiring a need for its affirmation but also resenting that he felt such a need. While he had come to feel comfortable holding his own in the guild, even that comfort made him a bit uncomfortable. Few of these folks knew his truly humble beginnings and how growing up on the margins had contributed to his prophetic imagination that offered an alternative to the reality that lay in front of him. This is why he was so drawn to Marx and liberation theology that spoke to the injustices of the marginalized in a way that neither the church nor the academy did so. Both had been domesticated by royal consciousness and coopted by the dominant society. Committed to both, Brueggemann was also a critic of both. Brueggemann recognized that his discomfort and disequilibrium of being marginalized went back to his childhood. Yet he also knew this position on the edge balancing opposites in a dance of disequilibrium always came with the prophetic call. He had experienced few days of equilibrium throughout his life.

Brueggemann's thoughts came back to the present. Whether in the church or the academy the fire burned in his bones—a fire that was always called for whatever the situation he found himself facing. Tonight's lecture would be no different because Brueggemann could not deviate from who he was called to be. At this moment, he would need the courage that Bernard Anderson had modeled for him. Brueggemann breathed a prayer of gratitude for his father August, his mentor Anderson and for the courage he knew would meet him at the lectern that evening as he gave the presidential address to a standing-room-only crowd of both admirers and detractors. He threw his legs over the side of the bed and started his day.

CLASSIC BRUEGGEMANN

Walter's presidential address was exactly what folks had come to expect from Brueggemann but even a bit more on that evening. Presidential addresses typically provided an opportunity for a scholar to assess their contribution to the field and to offer the audience some insight into how they saw their legacy. They were also often quite specialized, particularly in the last several decades. Specialization had come with all of higher education's increased rationality and had infected the SBL crowd also. The advantage of specialization for a conference paper presentation was that a presenter could use their subfield's unique jargon, reference a body of literature that only the specialists knew, and all the while sound convincing enough to prove that they deserved recognition. And by the time they were halfway through, there was the added advantage that most of the audience was either sleeping or imagining the desserts at the presidential reception that followed. But Brueggemann was intentionally more a generalist than a specialist, more a polytheist than a monotheist, and more a poet than a scientist. He wrote so that people in the back pew could understand. The last thing he wanted was the specialization that characterized so many other elite scholars to get in the way of what he was to share. He was determined that the "Amen" corner would stay awake that evening and the gluttons among the bunch would forget the desserts.

A generalist or interdisciplinary scholar, he took the text seriously but not literally. This had the added advantage of allowing Brueggemann to say things in such straightforward language that it stymied the specialists who were accustomed to taking language more literally than seriously. It also disturbed those siloed in their specialties that they had no idea what was happening anywhere else in the world. Brueggemann has already spawned an entire cottage industry of scholarship around what he intended by remarks such as "There is no God outside the text," "God's faithfulness is subverted by God's freedom," "God is hard to get," and "God has an unsettled inner being."

The evening continued to grind away with the one ax Brueggemann had been given—a prophetic imagination that revealed an "alternative to the reality that lay in front of God's people." The magic about this particular ax of Brueggemann, unlike other preachers who never stopped preaching the same message, is that by some stroke of genius the word he offered always sounded new and newly relevant to the time one was living in. But why not? This is precisely the same claim Brueggemann always made about the biblical text that he knew so well and took so very seriously if not literally. This taking the Bible seriously had nothing to do with discrediting literalists who took every word of the text to be God-breathed, nor did Brueggemann mean that as compared to detractors or other scholars he gave a serious reading of the text. What he meant came directly from his socialization in the German Evangelical Synod of North America where he had grown up repeatedly hearing "In essentials unity, in non-essentials liberty, and in all things charity." A Brueggemann rendering of a serious reading of the text was an assertion that one must allow the text freedom to speak on its own terms rather than assigning closed categories or meaning to it. Like so many riddles asked about Brueggemann, the answers lie in the past.

Brueggemann's title that night was "At the Mercy of Babylon: A Subversive Rereading of the Empire." Brueggemann's questions were: "What happens to speech about Babylon when it is drawn into the sphere of speech about God? And what happens to speech about God when it is drawn into the sphere of speech about the empire?"[3] What Brueggemann did that evening, whether the audience understood it or not, was to lead a Bible study and preach a sermon using the interdisciplinary tools of rhetorical analysis and social scientific interpretation—showing critical connections between the rhetoric across the Old Testament. Brueggemann led the audience through six different texts about Babylon, illustrating his unique grasp of the entire biblical canon and his incomparable capacity to see the arc of the story that held the passages together to yield previously invisible answers. The answers, in this case, are that God chooses to show mercy and to not show mercy and that the empire both shows mercy and receives mercy. Again he relied upon the prophetic imagination to reveal that what both Israel and Babylon assume to be true is not God's reality—God always has another based on God's imagination revealed to the prophet.

Brueggemann then shifted gears from Bible study mode to expressing gratitude to his beloved teacher James Muilenburg for directing the discipline from the flat and static historical-critical model to that of rhetorical analysis. He noted the importance of Muilenburg's 1968 presidential address in solidifying this movement. But he quickly revealed Muilenburg's contentment to stop with rhetorical analysis rather than venture further into the interpretation of the contemporary context, a move that Brueggemann made in extending his teacher's work.

Brueggemann had been a sociology major as an undergraduate at Elmhurst College and so the move into social interpretation was seamless, particularly given his voracious reading project that included many sociologists including Marx and Berger and more recently Ricoeur. In typical fashion, he was using his well-practiced exegetical move of making rhetorical connections, then layering that with sociology and topping it off with a layer of theology.

That evening, out of his critique of Muilenburg, he carefully made the second move and did so by citing the SBL presidential address of 1987 by Elizabeth Schussler Fiorenza in which she argued that every SBL address since 1880—with two exceptions—was always driven by scholarly detachment, and she was having none of that.[4] Hers would be the third address arguing for recognition of the public rhetoric of the text and Brueggemann's at least the fourth. The text demands a public response and a response of advocacy, they both argued.

Brueggemann's move to advocacy in his lecture was driven by his reading of Karl Marx and liberation theology, a reading that influenced *The Prophetic Imagination* in 1978 but became a commitment that was growing within Brueggemann, who believes that he came late to the game in terms of advocacy for women and other marginalized voices. But he was quickly making up for lost time and that was evident by where he was going next. He argued that the text must be read in light of China's Tiananmen Square and Berlin's Wall, of Panama's Canal and South Africa's apartheid, of Kuwait's lure for oil. This was a classic Brueggemann move— always stepping into the contemporary context but never without the biblical text in hand. No social justice advocacy is without the Bible and never the Bible without advocacy for the poor and marginalized.

And then, as usual, showing that nothing is sacred and siding directly with Fiorenza, he challenged his discipline's own form of status-grabbing: "Or among us, when we are daring, we may read the text in relation to the politics of publication, the play of power in promotion and tenure, the ambiguities of grantsmanship, and the seductions of institutional funding. We inevitably read the text where we sit."[5] Whether he recognized it at the time or not, this invocation that "where we sit" makes a difference in what we see was directly out of the playbook of early feminist Dorothy Smith, known for her conceptual apparatus of standpoint theory in which she had learned, as the only woman in Berkeley's 1960s sociology program, that where one sits makes all the difference in one's access to all the academy's goods that Brueggemann had just critiqued.[6] While Smith went home and changed diapers and took care of bloody noses, her male peers never differentiated home life from work life in the way that was required for women.

The standpoint of men and women, Smith insisted, also called for a methodology that allowed the voices of women to be expressed in authentic and genuine ways when gathering data. This meant the replacement of surveys with stories and songs that captured the experience of marginality in ways that numeric data as measurement outcomes could not. Smith's argument mirrored that of W. E. B. Du Bois, the Harvard-trained African American sociologist who recognized that the objectivity promised by quantitative research was not objective at all—it simply used the language of the dominant society to capture the reality of the dominant society that was not real or dominant for those on the margins. Both were calling for nothing less than a version of rhetorical analysis that emancipated the text of the voices of the marginalized from the dominant culture just as Brueggemann called for freeing the text from closed categories of historical criticism. Both were calling for the liberation of the texts! Fiorenza, and by extension Brueggemann, were following the lead of both Smith and Du Bois, as well as other scholars on the margins who grabbed ahold of Marx's analyses of class conflict, power, and inequality and integrated social justice advocacy into their sociological and prophetic imagining.

Behind the ballroom lectern, Brueggemann continued to challenge his colleagues but now as if he were preaching to the church: "The spillover of the text into present reality is not an 'add-on' for relevance, but it is a scholarly responsibility that the text should have a hearing as a serious voice on its own terms." Then notching things up a bit he found his prophetic voice: "Is it possible that we would be the generation that withholds the text from our contemporary world in the interest of objectivity and in the name of our privileged neutrality? . . . Such 'objective' and 'neutral' readings are themselves political acts in the service of entrenched and 'safe' interpretation."[7]

Brueggemann was grinding his ax in front of a crowd that he well knew had been the objective keepers of the text for decades. And while Muilenburg and his students—Brueggemann, Gottwald, and Trible among an increasing number of others—were changing the trajectory of their field, enough of the old guard remained for Brueggemann to know that not everyone appreciated his post-critical approach. Brueggemann himself had laid the groundwork over the last two decades for his ascendancy to the presidency of the SBL. And yet as one listened to him, one recognized that this award was more than a validation of his work by his peers, it was also a chance to do what he did best—preach prophetically to peers, speak truth to power, pile on the guilt, hope for some souls to be convicted, and then end it all with an altar call:

> It can, however, be otherwise. Without diminishing the importance of our critical work, it is possible that the text will be permitted freedom for its own fresh say. . . . The possibility of a fresh reading requires attentiveness to the politics of rhetoric, the strange, relentless power of these words to subvert and astonish. When our criticism allows the rhetoric of the text, the way mercy

crowds Babylon continues to be a crucial oddity, even in our own reading. Those of us who care most about criticism may attend with greater grace to the readings of the text that move beyond our own criticism.[8]

One wonders if anyone in the room that evening, besides undoubtedly Brueggemann, actually heard what he was insinuating—that he had finally arrived at the pinnacle of prestige of the SBL, only to find (though he likely knew already) that the SBL, like Babylon or Israel, was capable of receiving mercy if it extended mercy to the text and the marginalized and just as likely to receive judgment if it offered judgment to the text and the marginalized. And which one chose had everything to with one's imagination.

Brueggemann had just ground the ax of prophetic imagination for the hometown crowd as clearly as ever. He didn't flinch or falter, divert or dally, punt or protect. He was as much as ever the Jeremiah that folks had come to expect. He had been courageous or perhaps courage had shown up as he needed it. But like Babylon and so often God's people, one wonders if anyone was changed that night by Brueggemann's prophetic word. Did anyone go to bed after the presidential reception and lie awake wondering how they might change their research agenda, or how they might offer a hand to a marginalized colleague far outside the Old Boys' Club, or even become more engaged in their local community with those on the margins? If SBL members were anything at all like so many who come to hear a celebrity, they stood and clapped vigorously, then went to the bar for a drink and back to their rooms and turned on the television. The next day they would fly home with their prized autograph copy of one of Brueggemann's latest books to show their students before placing it along with two dozen other books on their "soon to read" shelf. Then they would turn in their receipts from the trip—including for the Brueggemann book—to the dean for reimbursement. Finally, they would add an item to their CV that reads "Presented a scholarly manuscript at the 1990 annual meeting of the SBL, New Orleans, Louisiana." Or "Paper in process entitled 'A Critical Review of Brueggemann's Criticism of Historical-Critical Analysis.'" These two items alone would ensure that they would get their pay raise next year.

Brueggemann went to bed aware of this reality—he had been in the church long enough to know how most receive a prophetic imaginer! But courageous he had been nonetheless.

AHEAD OF OR BEHIND HIS TIME?

It has been suggested that Brueggemann was ahead of his time.[9] But given that the SBL was formed in 1880 and over a century later was still not entirely ready to hear Brueggemann's word, one might wonder if the appearance of Brueggemann being ahead wasn't simply because, like most scholarship, that of the SBL was just so far behind as to make it appear that Brueggemann was radically ahead. Brueggemann was simply calling his discipline—as he was the church—back to the Bible and to free the text from the constraints that the Enlightenment had placed upon it. The constraints of historical criticism had become a noose around the discipline's capacity to offer "anything meaningful to the church" in Brueggemann's words.

Brueggemann did not consider himself to have discovered something novel or revolutionary in his reading of the biblical text. Instead, he was simply recovering what it means to live by faith. He understood that his call to free the text to a fresh reading was what occurred in every period of reform—whether it was Ezra or Jeremiah or Jesus or Luther or King. And while it has also been suggested that *The Prophetic Imagination* was a book ahead of Brueggemann that he would keep unpacking, it is equally true that *The Prophetic Imagination* was simply a prophet's call back to the Book that lay behind him. August Brueggemann's selection of "Thy Word is a lamp unto my feet and a light unto my path" (Psalm 119:105) for a life verse at his son's confirmation was no coincidence apparently for a son who would spend his life calling both the church and the academy back to the Bible.

SPECIALISTS WITHOUT SPIRIT

Writing in Germany in 1904, sociologist Max Weber predicted that the ongoing development of the modern world would lead to a loss of creativity and mystery. He called it disenchantment. Brueggemann called it a loss of imagination. Life would lose its mystery and beauty under the scrutiny of critical analysis. Counting things and predicting and controlling things would become the end rather than the means. Rationality would be institutionalized in bureaucracy, and society would find itself trapped in the "iron cage of rationality" and "mechanized petrification," all the while assuming that it was the height of superiority. The entire bureaucratic apparatus would be managed by "specialists without spirit" and "sensualists without heart."[10] The critical theorists writing in Germany during the Third Reich would extend Weber's critique and add to it Marx's voice as they attempted to understand the rise of authoritarian regimes in their day and the role of rationality in the efficient functioning of Hitler's death machinery. The answers lay in the Enlightenment and by extension in the science of race and eugenics spawned in the academies of the United States.[11]

Did Weber offer hope for a trapped society and its trapped institutions, including the church, academy, and even scholarly societies like the SBL? Yes, freedom, Weber suggested would only be discovered with the "rise of charismatic prophets" and the identification of old ideals. In other words, the answer for Weber was not in going forward but by going back, not by creating more scholarly societies or academic committees but by unleashing the voice of those courageous enough to call for the reconsideration of the old ideals. This was Brueggemann's lifelong call—to serve as a prophet to challenge the "taken-for-granted realities" of the church and the academy and to call for an alternative reality of emancipation that was true to the biblical text and the God of the text. His presidential address to the SBL could just as well have been spoken to a group of pastors at a church conference.

THE FIVE CORE TEXTS—ONE IMAGINATION

As Brueggemann reflects on the more than one hundred books that he authored across half a century, he boils them all down in terms of the central themes that captured his agenda to five works—*The Prophetic Imagination, Finally Comes the Poet, Psalms and the Life of Faith, An Old Testament Theology,* and *Money and Possessions.* While Brueggemann's thinking and awareness evolved across these five, the one feature that he argues holds them all together is the heuristic device of prophetic imagination—"seeing an alternative to one that lies in front of us."

The Prophetic Imagination

This now classic book is at the core of cores for Brueggemann. He sees it simply as the call for the church to return to the faith of their fathers and mothers. For one rooted in German evangelical pietism—ecumenical and irenic—it is a call to consider again the age-old story of the Bible that led Abraham to respond to an alternative reality than the one that lay in front of him. It is the imagination of Jeremiah to see God's judgment long before anyone else but also the first to see God's call for mercy for the Babylonian captors. And it was Jeremiah who saw that the empire was capable of unexpected mercy. The prophetic imagination always subverts the taken-for-granted reality of both captor and captive and reveals a God who is free from the socially constructed realities that keep God from being a free deity, domesticated in the image of God's people rather than God's people accepting the gentle domestication of their God. *The Prophetic Imagination* is a book calling for the reform of the church.

Finally Comes the Poet

Brueggemann gave the substance of this book in the Beecher Lectures at Yale Divinity School and "loves it for the simple exposition of texts in trying to argue that preaching should not be didactic, but that it should be an act of imagination that keeps opening out the world to new possibilities of God's governance"—certainly connected to *The Prophetic Imagination* but with a focus on the preaching of that imagination.[12]

Theology of the Old Testament: Testimony, Dispute, Advocacy

In this massive effort, which shows the depth and breadth of Brueggemann's knowledge of the biblical canon, he utilizes the metaphor of a courtroom to analyze the Old Testament texts.[13] The dialectic movement between core testimony and countertestimony as occurs in a courtroom is used to illustrate God's ongoing dialogic relationship with God's people.

> The core testimony of Israel is faith and counter-testimony is the hidden layers of God's testimony. We have to see that God is a very complex character who cannot be easily subsumed in any particular adjective. That God has a spectrum of emotional responses of which God is capable, which is another act of imagination. God has available a spectrum of emotive responses and reactions that cannot be reduced to any creedal summary.[14]

Psalms and the Life of Faith

Brueggemann's nearly career-long exegesis of the Psalms will likely be considered his most important contribution to the church.[15] His formation of the threefold typology of orientation, disorientation, and reorientation by which to interpret the Psalms has become the dominant exegetical mode for studying the Psalms. This device becomes another lens by which to see the alternative reality that can be otherwise missed if one is using historical-critical approaches that too often lead the reader's head to a greater understanding of the original historical context but their heart unmoved within their own present situation.

But as Brueggemann considers what he most wants to be remembered for in terms of his contribution overall, it is his writing about the Psalms of lament. They are "the script for an ongoing conversation with God. I think I have helped the church rediscover the lament songs after the church worked hard to get rid of them. The lament songs are the voice of faith, the voice of Israel. So that our conversation with God is a genuine dialogue and not a one-way address from God to us." As so much of one's theology is grounded in one's biography, so the lament Psalms reflect Brueggemann's own years in prayer and wrestling with God:

> I think lament Psalms have funded a great deal of my own prayer life and my own understanding of God, that this is a God who can be impinged upon and impacted and changed by our prayers, and that means that God must be perceived in quite Jewish ways of dialogue. Which makes me very nervous when you get the theological categories of omniscience and omnipotence and omnipresence. I think that the dialogic covenant and interactive model is defining for me, and the Psalms basically express that. They continue to deconstruct our false certitudes.[16]

Brueggemann hopes that his work will result in lament Psalms permeating the life and liturgy of the church. He believes that he is singularly responsible for that.

Money and Possessions[17]

In this most recent of the five books, Brueggemann explores how the Bible is preoccupied with economic questions. He has come to understand that being at the margins of the economy is related to one's capacity for the prophetic imagining of an alternative reality. Being at the center of the economy, one assumes that everything is given and settled and thus there is no room for imagination nor desire for imagination beyond the status quo. Those in the center of the economy need only know one story—their own. Those on the margins have to know two stories, their own and that of those in the center—sometimes one's life depends on knowing both. The economic engine has become increasingly important to Walter: "I do not want to be a liberal hack, but I want to insist that the Bible's thinking about economics is an act of imagination nowhere clearer than in Jesus's parable where he paid for workers in the ninth hour, the same as the third. The power of this parable is in being an intrusion into economic reality."[18] An awareness of the margins increased in volume for Brueggemann over the years but was intrinsic "I think from the beginning" of his life as he considers their family's marginality in Blackburn and his awareness of and engagement with the small Black community in their hometown.

Brueggemann sees the continuity among these five books as being that of the prophetic imagination and the change across time being his growing emphasis on the place of economic issues in Scripture: "I don't think it's changed a lot, but I think it has tilted much more toward the economic. In my later and my more recent work, I am in a very simple-minded way convinced of Marx's class analysis and that it's always the haves and the have-nots. And I think that has continued to develop for me."

These five works, like his others, share the assumption that the Bible requires us to do interpretation that is not domesticated or dictated by the dominant assumptions of our society since the Old and New Testaments are the Scriptures of the church and as such must have meaning that is not fixed in traditions. Relevant meaning for the contemporary church can and must be discovered ever anew.

A WORD TO THE POWERS

Concerns for social justice and economic equity have been within Walter since childhood. He never forgot the abuse he saw his father August experience as a pastor—the economic injustice, the marginalization within church and community, and so poorly esteemed. His father carried on with courage—he worked eighty-hour weeks, was always on call, and endured severe criticism of his efforts to modernize the church and to make the Gospel relevant to young people. But it was also being faced with the discrimination of Black neighbors in Blackburn, Missouri, that revealed another kind of injustice to Walter. Justice was ascribed by the color of one's skin. The kind that oppressed an entire group of people. The kind that had been socially constructed by the dominant society for the subjugation of that society. The kind that once ascribed there was no getting out or going upward. The kind that is based on caste rather than class.

Brueggemann has long seen justice as central to the heart of God, but his commitment to that belief has intensified over the decades as he has observed the world around him—reading two or three newspapers each day—and as he has remained deeply and daily within the biblical text. He just kept coming up again and again to the centrality that justice has within God's economy. He recognized the injustice with which the church treated his father as a pastor. He recognized the injustice of Black residents of Blackburn with whom he and his brother Ed worshipped.

At Elmhurst College, he was quiet in the classroom and his sociology professor Theophil Mueller was a curmudgeon who did not engage with students. Yet Walter took eight courses from him, and central to Mueller's long lectures was the theme of racial and economic injustice experienced by the marginalized in American society. The work of Karl Marx was not on Mueller's radar at this point just as it was not on the radar of most American sociologists. Nonetheless, Mueller was an activist for racial justice who integrated his strong views into the classroom. Regardless of the course, he found ways to incorporate economic and social justice concerns—in Rural Sociology he addressed land concerns and in Urban Sociology concerns about housing and in Criminology the increased mass incarceration of Black men.

It was really through his introduction to Mexican author José Miranda's book *Marx and God* that most sensitized Walter to the realities of injustice and marginality. He neither remembers when and where or how this book came to him, but it had a powerful impact. Writing from the global periphery in 1971, Miranda does a thorough exegesis of the biblical text to arrive at his conclusions even as he acknowledges his reliance upon Karl Marx. Miranda makes connections between both the Old and New Testaments in a style, not unlike Brueggemann himself. Miranda argues that the Kingdom of God can only exist where justice rules the earth. Miranda was so useful because he showed how the essentials of a Marxist critique were all present in the prophetic tradition. Walter had not seen that connection before. At the same time, Walter team-taught an interdisciplinary course at Eden Seminary with his good friend and colleague Professor Douglass Meeks.

From Meeks, he learned Marxian economic criticism. Meeks had studied Marx in Europe and was influenced by Habermas, the Frankfurt School, and others.

Walter had already been postured in the direction of God's justice since childhood, but Miranda's method of exegesis and Meeks's tutoring resonated with him. Walter would continue to read widely in the literature of liberation theology at just the time when the social sciences were also moving toward neo-Marxist and conflict perspectives. As one who depended upon sociological interpretation as part of his own exegetical mode, the dual movements within both theology and sociology toward Marx helped to push Brueggemann in the same direction. He would become an early leader in biblical studies and theology to apply consistently to the biblical text a conflict perspective that considered God's concern with justice for all those on the margins. And Brueggemann's confidence that the text and its God were continually opening to reveal new responses to social, economic, and religious realities meant that he more quickly than others embraced gay ordination, the inclusion of women in all levels of the church, and a focus on the outsider. Walter did not hesitate to cross such lines, not because he sensed it was politically or ecclesiastically expedient, but because his exegesis of the text led him to these marginalized voices.

This would remain a quality by which Walter's work would be known and that would set him up to lead pastors and churches beyond theological quarrels that would last for decades and that continue today. His desire to move quickly beyond quarrels was undoubtedly led by his faith tradition's origins in the Prussian Union which was based on the pragmatic decision by Prince Frederic in 1817 to merge Calvinists and Lutherans. The trajectory of Brueggemann's positions can always be traced back to his childhood grounding in the Evangelical Synod of North America, to his father, his wide reading across disciplines, and his collegial engagement with other scholars, who as conversation partners he has allowed to inform his work.

As if to remind the church that in addition to his many books based upon the book of Jeremiah, Brueggemann released another in 2022 entitled *Returning from the Abyss: Pivotal Moments in the Book of Jeremiah.*[19] As with all his work, this book is both ancient and contemporary, both theology and sociology, both a word for the church and the empire and especially in this season when the church has allowed itself to be absorbed into the empire so easily. So that to be a Christian is to embrace a royal consciousness of exclusion of the marginalized from the middle, for example people of color from access to resources that could begin to create equity. White supremacy and white oppression thrive only in an empire held together by deception. A theology of the oppressed that is true to God's central concern for the poor is radically different from a theology of the privileged, which is white and nationalistic.

The older Walter has become and the longer he has written, the more directly and courageously and openly he has addressed the politics of oppression. But he never does so from a theology-lite position. He just seems more and more concerned for a church that looks increasingly like the white nationalism of the German Third Reich. And he comes out of a tradition that engaged with the Confessing Church of Germany and that came down solidly on the side of God's righteous judgment on the evils of dehumanization and objectivation of the other. The influence of the Confessing Church and its pastor-scholars upon Brueggemann cannot be overstated. Both his theology and social conscience reflected its influence.

Superpowers are quite transient. In their wealth and power and hubris, they imagine themselves to exist in perpetuity—like the Third Reich for a thousand years. Prophetic faith attests otherwise. Not even the wealthiest, most powerful superpower can outflank God. The sinking of Babylon is permanent and irreversible: "Rise no more!" . . . Superpowers, however, keep learning this truth belatedly as did the United States in Vietnam, as did the Soviet Union in Afghanistan, as is the United States most recently in Afghanistan. History is not finally or fully subject to absolute human control. There is always a wild card. Israel's name for that improbable wild card is "YHWH . . . ."[20]

A SOCIOLOGICAL IMAGINATION?

Brueggemann has been lauded for his particular knack for creating typologies or theological apparatuses through which to sort and sift and see and frame biblical truth—point and counterpoint, pivots, orientation, disorientation, and reorientation, and structural legitimation and embrace of pain, among others. What many miss is that Brueggemann is drawing upon sociological tendencies since Weber to create "ideal types" to explain social realities—not as predictive categories as Durkheim used them but as tools or frames by which to clarify social realities. Weber's goal was to understand from the subjective level of the actor the meaning that the actor assigned to certain experiences, rather than to impose meaning on the actor, as opposed to Émile

Durkheim, who sought to explain and predict human behavior through the creation of causal categories. Historical criticism had done the same thing. Durkheim's theories of structural-functionalism reinforced that status quo and assumed equilibrium and offered no theory of change. Historical criticism functioned to do about the same.

Among sociologists in the United States, Durkheim's theories reigned through the 1950s. But the social movements of the 1960s and 1970s would send sociologists running in the direction of Marx and conflict theories to understand what was occurring in American society and to address the failure of their discipline to incorporate the realities of the marginalized, including members of its own guild, including Dorothy Smith and W. E. B. Du Bois. A major realignment took place within sociology, and as one who was a sociologist before he was a theologian and as one who read widely across disciplines, Brueggemann was aware of this shift and began to weave it into his theology far earlier than most of his peers.

Following the completion of his undergraduate degree at Elmhurst College, Brueggemann went directly to Eden Seminary in 1954, a seminary known since Richard Niebuhr was dean in the late 1920s and early 1930s as the "seminary of sociology." This term was associated with Niebuhr's push to dramatically change the small seminary's posture from a sectarian, inward-looking institution to one with an outward engagement with the world. This resulted in curriculum additions such as psychology and philosophy, among others. The new alignment did not come without conflict and testing of the ethos that would define Eden Seminary. It would take the termination of two newly appointed German faculty members to solidify the Niebuhr influence upon

Eden as the seminary of sociology. Though vindicated by the seminary's board of directors, Richard would leave Eden Seminary for Yale. Still, both he and his brother H. Reinhold—who chaired the Seminary Board for twenty-five years—would yield substantial influence on the seminary for decades to come. And Brueggemann would be the first to formally fill Richard's shoes when he was appointed dean in 1968. No one was more prepared for those shoes than Brueggemann, whose ethos and outlook were so similar and had come from the same deep German Evangelical well of ecumenism, pietism, and an irenic posture of "in essentials unity, in non-essentials liberty, and in all things charity."

In the mid-twentieth century, sociologist C. Wright Mills introduced the sociological imagination as a concept by which one comes to recognize that the macro-level forces of society shape what happens at the micro-level.[21] This reality demands an understanding of how one's individual problems and experience reflect the macro-level forces that are pressing down on all of us. Peter Berger uses the metaphor of puppets and puppeteers to illustrate the idea more precisely. Sociology is useful, says Berger, in calling upon individuals to take the courage to look up into the stage ceiling and identify who and what is pulling their strings. "And this," says Berger, "is the first step toward freedom."[22]

Brueggemann's prophetic imagination demands that the church and academy see themselves as they indeed are—domesticated by forces that constrain, coopt, capture, and confine—so that both might take freedom's first step. He has sought to emancipate the text, the God of the text, and the text's readers. And perhaps in the process has been emancipated a bit himself.

FOUR

Pivoting Here and There

Every pivot was a turn from moralism to freedom.
Walter Brueggemann

Marc Nelesen lay his head on the table in Heckman Library and slept. So much reading. So little time for reflection. Was seminary meant to train future pastors not to reflect? Marc had begun his journey at Calvin Theological Seminary, hoping to expand and explore, knowing this only happens through engaging more deeply. He would seek something relevant as well as something to address future difficulties in ministry. He enjoyed the intellectual stimulation of his systematic theology courses but also yearned for something that would inspire and ignite his heart. In his time, seminary could bend toward being more academic, detached, and cool rather than engaged and warming.

AWAKENED

He slowly woke and recognized his surroundings. He had one more required book to read before the mid-term. This one was different from the rest. At the time, Marc didn't have categories for evangelical or progressive, but

this book was written by the latter not the former. The
author of this book was more concerned with social
justice than Jesus. The author's one planned lecture at
Calvin College had been canceled—long before cancel
culture was a thing. The faculty had concerns about
his theology. The author's name was Brueggemann—
probably a descendant from one of those freethinking
German liberals. And a graduate of Union Theological Seminary—about as far theologically from Calvin
as New York City is from Grand Rapids. But being a
diligent student, Marc would try to read tonight in the
comfort of his home (or own surroundings). He pulled
his things together and left the library.

But that evening, a change occurred within Marc
that would last forever. Something was activated in
him. That transformation would save his life years later.
As he read Brueggemann's short, required paperback,
The Land, something resonated deeply within him.
Was it the author's spirit? Or his love of the text? Or
his insight into who or what lay behind the text? The
unusually high view of Scripture and the fervor of the
Spirit's life that pulsated through the book felt so Calvinist. "Heart, energy, fire, life—the ruah that always
seemed to frighten the cognitive folks, including his
professors," Marc thought to himself.

The following day Marc excitedly raced to his
professor's office and met up with him in the hallway.
He couldn't wait to share what had happened to him.
He expressed gratitude for the Brueggemann reading.
Marc even insinuated, partly in jest, that he'd had a
conversion experience. His professor listened. Lower-
ing his head and looking over the top of his glasses,
he urged caution. "Be careful with him." His words
communicated warning and some concern that Marc
should be more discerning. Marc looked down. He was

quiet. He had just experienced God in the most mean-ingful way yet since coming to Calvin. It was the kind of encounter with God that he had hoped was a regular experience for seminarians. He was confused. The very book and author that was required reading was now being regarded with some caution. It felt like mixed messaging. Marc was disappointed, perplexed, and a bit astonished as the words ran against his own experience.

The professor seemed satisfied with both the cor-rective and the retroactive warning label he put on Brueggemann's book. He had no choice. Brueggemann's textual apparatuses and higher criticism were suspect among most evangelicals. And, certainly, Brueggemann wasn't a Calvinist—he belonged to the UCC. Marc looked up. Startling his professor, he thanked him for introducing him to Brueggemann. Watching the pro-fessor's jaw twitch, Marc assured him that he would be looking into everything Brueggemann ever wrote. And indeed, he did so—and Walter's work sustained his spiritual and emotional life throughout the remainder of seminary.

Marc would later see the irony of Brueggemann being so easily dismissed at Calvin College. In so many ways, he was an archetype of John Calvin. Calvin, like Brueggemann, taught that one had to be open with one-self to know God. Walter was as thoroughly Calvinist as anyone at the seminary, if not more so. Even his pro-motion of social justice concerns reflected more Calvin than Luther.

SAVED

Marc was ordained in 1996 and began his ministry at Third Christian Reformed Church. But by 2002, he was raw and at the end of his tether following a series of community tragedies, suicides, sudden deaths, and significant personal losses. "At the end" meant many things, including ministry, God, and potentially his own life. Each had turned on him and left him wounded. As if 9/11 was not enough, that same week, a neighborhood mother killed her children. Marc was already at the intersection of darkness and light. With the death of these children, he pivoted toward darkness. He was ready to end his own life.

On May 17, he walked into Fourth Presbyterian Church in Chicago. Walter was preaching, and *The Secret of Survival* was the title. Marc had given up on quick fixes and self-help books a long time ago, and he was pretty sure he had tried every secret already. But if anyone could yet channel hope from the biblical text to his trauma, it was Brueggemann. Brueggemann preached from Jeremiah 20:7–23. As he did so often, he boldly and dramatically embodied the prophet Jeremiah and the God of the prophet. He looked at the audience with prophetic passion and pastoral compassion above his reading glasses. He delivered a message of three parts consolation and one part challenge. He gave out of what he needed to hear himself that morning. He marked out Jeremiah's various pivots as the prophet wrestled with a deceptive and scandalous God. A God who gave him no choice but to proclaim violence and destruction upon Israel. He had tried to beg himself out of the call. After all, he was just a child. Why did this deity always choose the little people, called as children, to do the biggest jobs? Moses in the bull rushes? Samuel in the temple? David, the youngest, missing from the lineup of brothers who might be king? Joash the seven-year-old to reform Israel? John the Baptist? Their lot was determined in the heavens long before birth, their destiny written in the stars. For a free God—that God offered little freedom to those chosen to do the down and dirty work of bringing reform.

The outcome of obedience for Jeremiah? Get hammered by the religious bureaucrats who had pivoted away from God long ago. Jeremiah had been given no choice in the matter. As a child, God met him and said, "You will pluck up and tear down. And you will come against the royal empire and its apparatus." So Jeremiah did what good kids do. They obey and conform to and keep the rules. And he paid for it—finding himself in a dark cistern looking up at the light. He had pivoted from light to darkness without any say in the matter. Marc could identify. Neither life nor ministry nor the world was working according to the scripts offered by systematic theology. Neither was God and that was part of the crisis.

In many ways, this was Jeremiah's crisis too. When he tried to stop this idiotic proclamation of death and destruction that sentenced him to the cistern, his bones burned up. Like rheumatoid arthritis. Like spinal stenosis. Like a broken femur. Pain within or pain without? Which did he prefer? YHWH had cornered him and boxed him in. The One who called had now gone silent. Jeremiah was deeply wounded by it all—paralyzed at a crossroads that was no crossroads at all.

Jeremiah's response and the secret to his survival? Get in God's face. Get down and dirty with God. Demand that God look at God's duplicitous self in the mirror! Tell God to be God or else! Put God in God's own box! Make a point of reminding God of God's own offenses before God gets a chance to get back up and deliver a counterpoint. Pivot from one corner of YHWH's box to the next. Stay one step ahead. Beat God to his own pivot or pivot before God can. Offer

God a right uppercut but throw him off with a left side hook.

Then, after utter exhaustion and putting God in God's place, Jeremiah is emptied enough to finally hear the divine whisper, "I am with you." Jeremiah wasn't ready to hear that deep truth because he had deep truths of pain and hurt and abandonment that needed to be told. Before that, his temptation was to bear false witness against those hurts that ran so deep. He dares not admit these to himself let alone before God. But then he reached a point where he *had* to because there was no other place to go. Deep hurts told to God made the occasion for newness. The adversaries were the same, but Jeremiah was transformed. The powerful pivot of the text was that YHWH moved from being an enemy to an ally. God had promised to make him a "fortified city, an iron pillar, and a bronze wall." Nobody, including the church bureaucrats, or the kings or priests, could defeat him. For a moment, Jeremiah had forgotten the promises of God that had come with his call. God had made him a warrior.

As Jeremiah remembers, he moves from private prayer to public doxology and full-blown praise. His enemies were mere fleas, nothing to be feared. His false prophet peers who had forgotten how to dance or wrestle with God would never get to genuine doxology. Their lack of private pathos resulted in public lies. For the pathway to praise was through the private boxing match he just had with God. Getting in God's face had released remembrance, had moved Jeremiah from fear of the day of his death to a vital faith by recollecting his calling.

The pivot of Jeremiah from private pathos to authentic public praise hit Marc hard. Pastors need to engage God deeply in secret. This is the "Secret to Survival." Marc had been hanging onto what was left of life by traveling, therapy, retreats, and continuing education experiences. All good, but not good enough. He had missed the part about telling God how awful God had been to not fit within the systematic boxes he learned so well. Those boxes didn't have room to tell God how cruel, unfair, deceptive, unkind, and abandoning he was. You don't do that with God—or at least you shouldn't. The fences urging appropriate safety cautions around God had been well learned.

But then Marc remembered his first encounter with Brueggemann. How limiting he had found systematic theology at the time. How fresh and refreshing he had found this risky and dangerous prophet who saw nothing systematic about the text or the God of the text. Who saw that God as a free agent but more, as wild and woolly and who did willy-nilly whatever God wanted to do. Neither the circumstances nor the categories could limit or define God.

This was the God Marc needed now. Not a nice but neutered God made predictable by systems and categories stuck in the nineteenth century. Nor a God who told us to do good things but left us powerless to do them. As Marc left that morning, he had heard consolation—not condemnation. More comfort than conviction. He experienced a God who could take all that Marc had to give him and even *welcomed that kind of engagement.* And with it came not an iota of condescension. Preachers who have gone to war with God before stepping into the pulpit cannot be condescending to their listeners. They are too tired. Too broken. Too wounded. All of which have brought them to a place of greater grace for God, for themselves, and their listeners. There are no prophets unbroken.

Marc left that morning hearing Brueggemann's promise that those who followed the secret script of Jeremiah's prayer would soar like eagles. He drove home, knowing that he had pivoted back toward light! He would survive! He let out a deep belly laugh, a laugh that had been hiding under the pain. Brueggemann had set a captive free by naming the hard things, and that captive was Marc. Walter had intersected with Marc's raw heartache and had restored Marc's confidence in God.

DOWN AND DIRTY WITH GOD

Of course, Marc knew, as did anyone else that day who had ever experienced an aching heart, that only those who knew agony could preach of freedom, the way that Walter did so. Clearly, like Jeremiah and Marc, the prophet Brueggemann was walking through his own down-and-dirty moment with God. Feeling the sting of God's deception. Running from accusations by those who pigeonholed him. Running from misunderstandings by those who didn't engage in relationships with their entire beings. Running from those intolerant of God's wild and free "otherness." Rejected by those who lived with closed categories that protected them from intimacy. A suspect among those who feared the hell of life at intersections of light and darkness. Who preferred moralism over freedom.

Brueggemann could preach of Jeremiah's abandonment because he was there himself. He could preach of Jeremiah's loneliness because it was the loneliness of every true prophet. After all, that was his context—alone though surrounded by many. Brueggemann knew what it was to get into his prayer closet and to utter things to God that he would never utter to others. To use language with God in private that was acceptable only to God. With God, he could engage heresy while being held. He could drop the F-bomb with God and not lose his preaching credentials with the UCC bureaucrats. Such language reflected one's intimacy with God—it had been the disorientation and tears the night before that empowered Brueggemann's preaching this morning. Last night's journal entry of loneliness and hopelessness was the lens through which Walter saw the text anew the following day. Like many lonely prophets before him, he knew again that the Almighty saw him. It is no wonder that Walter Brueggemann resists it when others put him in boxes or categories.

And because he now knew he was seen, he could see those like Marc who showed up that morning with a plan to end it all. Walter connected with the pain of those in public because he had confronted God in private the night before. Everyone, like Marc, heard the message as if it were being shared specifically for them. And then, for a moment at least, Walter, Jeremiah, Marc, and those of their ilk, arrived at doxology. Brueggemann preached as someone who knew that the only secret to praise was to get in God's face and demand that God be God again. Marc had been trying to get to praise without addressing God honestly. Those who grow up with Jonathan Edwards's angry God so often fail to recognize why that God is angry—not at us but with those who teach us that God cannot handle our anger. That God is either fragile and needs to be treated with care or needs secret service protection from theological boundary violators who get too close. A God who is completely omniscient ends up being restricted from being able to pivot here and there—with us, for, and against us.

PIVOTS

Brueggemann had long loved the text of Jeremiah for the way it rocked and rolled from pivot to pivot. The way the text pivoted, God pivoted, and Jeremiah pivoted. If one reads the text with open eyes, it seems impossible to believe in an unchanging or changeless One. The book of Jeremiah is loaded with intersections and pivots and a God whose mind was ever-reversing and who gave every impression of having a troubled interior life! The book was packed with conditional clauses that suggested a free God, a free text, and a free prophet. The book is filled with polarities as if God were Black and white and light and dark. But at other times, he is a shadow living in shadows. And so, the prophet lives and prophecies in the shadows also. Walter did the same—creating typologies of polarities and denying that they applied to him. But a free prophet called by a free God gets a free pass to do so!

The book of Jeremiah is set up in a context of royal consciousness versus critical resentment grounded in God's covenant—empire versus temple and king versus priest. In 587 BCE, the Jewish exiles go into the abyss and seventy years later walk out of it—at least a few of them. Jeremiah's call was to pluck up and to plant, and he was as uncertain as his listeners which of these he was up to some days. "God is sending you into your worst nightmare in Babylon. Oh, by the way, make your home there and bring them the shalom you failed to offer the widows and orphans and aliens back home." The continual reminder of the covenant, "IF you return,

THEN God . . . " was a covenant until God said it wasn't because Israel could not keep the "if." Then God stepped in and changed the "then" of destruction promised. Perhaps Walter's favorite related passage is where God promises "to bring a full end" to God's people and then, in the next breath, says, "But I won't!" One gets the sense of God as a parent who promises and threatens. But, in the end, is free to retain the promise or threat or to throw it all away and start over again. One moment the kids are on the hook for their offense and the next moment they are off to sin again—with a trip for ice cream in between.

And indeed, Brueggemann's life represented one intersection after another. Intersections between wanting to be accepted by others and wanting to be his authentic self. Intersections of conformity and nonconformity. Intersections of his mother and father. Intersections of light and darkness. Intersections of moralism and freedom. He articulated his distress at these intersections through written prayers. He looked for answers in the biblical text. He sought out psychotherapy to guide him through these intersections. He read Freud and Winnicott. He tried to understand what drove him, and where the shame had come from. Why he worked so hard; why some relationships were so rewarding and others so difficult; why he felt so inadequate.

AWAY FROM MORALISM

Numerous pivot points dot Walter's lifelong landscape. He has spent a lifetime coming to terms with a mother who demanded conformity to the community's expectations for a preacher's family. For one called to the prophetic as a child—aware of it or not at the time—this was a pigeonhole he could hardly tolerate. His mother represented moralism—doing the right thing—he has spent a lifetime trying to escape. Prophets are rarely known for doing or saying the right thing. They are born with burning bones. They resist while coming through the birth canal. They protest injustice before anyone else. The last thing they can do is be good. The last thing God wants for them is to be good.

But she was so fearful that her sons would do something to rock the boat. To jeopardize their father's ministry. To call negative attention to themselves. There was a kind of invisibility that she demanded of her boys and even of her husband. Ministry without might. Prophecy without power. Grace without freedom. Love God and neighbor but only as they wish to be loved. "In all things conformity." No risks. No mistakes. No faults. No failures.

Walter fell in line with his mother. He never heard these concerns from his father. A father who took risks in demanding that the school board provide Latin instruction to his two boys. A father who crossed lines to meet with Black residents of Blackburn. A father who went to the home of the new Missouri Synod Lutheran pastor, but a pastor who refused to recognize August. A father who welcomed Missouri Synod members to St. Paul's UCC who were running from moralism to freedom. A father affectionately called "Pops" in the local conference for his ministry and mentoring of younger pastors. A father who insisted that the church give up German for the sake of the youth. A father who would have preferred gardening to guiding a flock.

Perhaps it was her husband's actions she was most anxious about but over which she had little control. The one person she could control was Walter. Because older brother Ed would have none of it! So Walter fell in line with his mother and tried to "always, always be good." To bury any desire for adventure. To be a good son. To be a good student. To be a good brother. To be a good graduate student. To be a good seminary professor. To be a good writer. To be good enough. But the constraints of moralism and conformity confined this prophet and made him tired. Brought him to his end many days. Caused him to be the last to leave the seminary at the end of the day. Walter would spend a lifetime trying to move from the moralism of his mother to the freedom and grace experienced with his father. A lifetime moving from the puritanical closed categories of his mother to the ecumenism and evangelical pietism of his father. A lifetime working to acquit himself of the shame he experienced as a constant voice inside his head. One hundred books later, he still wonders some days whether he has been good enough. He must work to stay in grace, but some days are now better than they used to be.

Walter's movement from moralism to freedom was helped by his study of Freud and those who adapted Freud's perspective. He began to see the chilling effect of a conformist society and the necessity of stepping out of that conformity for the sake of one's life. He found the writing of child psychiatrist D. W. Winnicott particularly helpful.[1] Winnicott concluded that for the first two years of life, the mother must let the child have the experience of omnipotence. The mother ignores bad behavior and just smiles at their indiscretions. But at age two, to not produce a monster, one must begin to withdraw omnipotence, or the child will become a teenager imagining she is still omnipotent. Of course, this was not Walter's childhood experience, but as he became aware of what he had missed, this new understanding began to release Walter from the conforming voice of his mother. The longer Walter understood this, the more time he spent in the Psalms of lament. He recognized them as a place where the author and the reader are given the space of a toddler—space to be omniscient in the face of God.

FOR THE CHURCH

Early in his career, Walter aspired to be like Harvey Cox. A household name. A hot shot. A bestselling author. A giant among his peers. He worked with defiance that would prove his worth to the world. He worked from behind but had his eyes far ahead. He sat in the back knowing by the end of the semester he would be at the front. His posture was more akin to vindication in his scholarship than to grace in his gifts. But slowly and with time the defiance and anger began to recede. As his national profile rose, he received numerous offers from research universities. In one case, responding to an invitation to teach at an Ivy League institution, he replied, "If I go there I will never think another original thought!"

But he began to discover that the church was his natural habitat, just as it had been for his father. Until that moment of acceptance, however, he had a tense relationship with the guild of big players in Old Testament studies. They did not think he was a real scholar. Too preachy. Too poetic. Not from the center. From Missouri for crying out loud. Who ever heard of Eden Seminary? The Evangelical Synod of North America had long ago been buried within the UCC. What possible good could come from Nazareth? Or from Anathoth? Or from Blackburn?

But he persisted in his exegetical approach that moved away from the historical form of criticism of

von Rad and others, and toward the freedom of rhetorical analysis and a more subjective interpretation.
The subjectiveness he sought was sociological—going
back to his undergrad days at Elmhurst College. It was
the subjectiveness of the actor in the text. The meaning
of the rhetoric in the text for the actor. This subjectiveness was understood and interpreted through the
rhetorical connections of the text. Words are symbols.
Symbols mean something to the actors. Brueggemann
fostered an exegetical method that began with plotting
the rhetorical connections, interpreting the subjective meaning, and wrapping the whole thing up with
theological questions: Where is God? What is God
doing? What if God's counterpoint? Where is God
going? Nobody else was doing this in the same way
and with such intentionality. And no one did it with
their eye on the meaning of the contemporary church
like Brueggemann.

Younger scholars began to gravitate toward
Brueggemann. Preaching and papers on preaching
became more acceptable at guild meetings like the SBL.
Scholars began to take more risks in doing work on
behalf of the church. A living God and a living text,
credited by some to be the influence of both Brevard
Childs and Walter Brueggemann, could now be heard
in the corridors and meeting rooms of professional meetings where once God had never been invited. Eventually, the tipping point between old and new paradigms
was reached. While it was not so clear what lay ahead, it
was obvious by 1990, when Walter was president of the
SBL, that there was no going back to what was.

Getting over the "disease" of the historical-critical
method was liberating. Not only did he give up trying
to be a scholar that he couldn't be, but he also embraced
the scholar he was meant to be. He moved from shame

to self-acceptance. The comfort of the church habitat and the result of embracing his call to that habitat would ultimately contribute to the massive productivity of the man. And by wiping the dust of erudite scholarship from his shoes, he was freed to move into the future newly oriented.

MOVING TOWARD MARX

The commitment that Brueggemann made early on to incorporate sociology into his exegesis meant that the relevance of his work would remain for the church. As he was writing in the 1960s and 1970s, shifting the paradigm of biblical studies to a more interpretive approach, sociology was also undergoing profound change. The structural-functional model that emerged from Émile Durkheim's work in France in the late nineteenth century was slowly being replaced by conflict and critical models derived from the work of Karl Marx in the mid-eighteenth century. Durkheim assumed that societies were inherently stable or in equilibrium. When stability was threatened, societies found ways to adapt and reestablish equilibrium. The model deemphasized change and offered no interpretive device for understanding how change occurs. Structural-functionalism tended to reinforce the status quo of society. The problem with Durkheim's model was that nothing seemed stable in America in the 1960s and 1970s. Change was certainly occurring. And the status quo appeared to be going to hell. In response, sociologists looked to Marx for answers. Marx assumed that society was always conflicted and banked on society's rejection of the status quo. He offered revolution as the mechanism for change. He recognized that power is always somewhere, and where it is and who has it can be a matter of life and death.

At the same time, Brueggemann began to read liberation theology, particularly the work of José Miranda. Immediately Miranda's ideas resonated with Walter. Marginalization of the poor, people of color, and even pastor families—Walter had seen some of this growing up. He and his family had experienced these realities at several levels. He began to read voraciously. If one went to the Eden Seminary's library to check out a book, Brueggemann's name was always already on the card as having checked it out. This was true about anything related to Marx for sure.

Walter now began to see conflict within every text. Every text had an ax to grind. Power was always at play. God's power. The king's power. The priests' power. Babylon's power. Imperial power. And suddenly Brueggemann began to see the economic themes that run through the biblical text. In a new way, he saw that God takes the marginalized, oppressed, and powerless. God creates conflict when the If–Then covenant is violated. God is the mechanism for change. God rewards the last with a banquet they didn't expect and sends the first to wash the dishes. This new neo-Marxist lens had immediate and practical implications for Brueggemann. In the 1970s he began to support the ordination of gay pastors. He got on board with the feminist movement. He became engaged more deeply in the civil rights movement. His shift was welcomed by progressives and liberals but little understood. His positions and perspectives came out of his understanding of the biblical text. The progressives too often had long ago decided that God did not matter. Progressives locked into nineteenth-century categories of developmentalism and evolution were uneasy about too much appeal to the old tradition. Evangelicals locked into categories of the eighteenth century felt betrayed and saw Brueggemann as increasingly suspect. But the dominance of the neo-Marxist and conflict models has meant that a new generation of scholars is finding Walter's work relevant, even as they extend themselves beyond where Walter has gone. They have Walter in large part to thank for making that extension possible.

JEWISH THEOLOGY

Walter also pivoted toward a Jewish theological understanding of the biblical text. A slow process, as all his pivots were, a primary Jewish influence on Brueggemann was Abraham Heschel. Heschel was a friend of Professor James Muilenburg, Brueggemann's Doctor Father at Union Theological Seminary. Walter began to figure out that Jewish scholars not only arrived at different conclusions but that Jewish interpretation proceeded in a very different way. Walter found this way of thinking about the biblical text to fit well with his own exegetical method. The goal was to simply review a text to see what it means—again that subjective understanding of the text for the actors but also for the reader. In some ways, the reader and the actor and God meet in a dialogical way to explore whatever text lies in front of them, with no pressure to fit the text into a scheme or compare it to an established doctrine or feel any pressure to draw certain conclusions. The more that Walter engaged the text this way, the longer he met the text with this posture, and the more he found it interesting and generative and endlessly open-ended.

Walter experienced the open-endedness of the Jewish text to be exhilarating and amazing. He was lured by the verdict of Robert Alter that Judaism is "a culture of interpretation," and wanted to find a way to participate in that lively culture.[2] The text and its God resist closure in Jewish theology. This was precisely what Brueggemann had been moving toward from the moment he became Muilenburg's student. Spending time in the text, one always found some part of the narrative that called into question the rest of the text. Discovering that the "footnote of openness" brings mystery and vitality and drama to the Bible. So that about the time one believes one has it all figured out, the text moves and God moves. Then one must start all over again from the beginning. But as one approaches the text again one does so with new awareness and begins looking for new movements and points and counterpoints. The revelation that the biblical text and the God of that text were more open-ended and less of a "moralist" that Brueggemann had long assumed opened the doors of his own life to greater freedom. This allowed him to live with a recognition that he has not yet arrived at a destination or an understanding. He no longer saw as many closures in the text or God, or his own life for that matter.

This brought him full circle back to the German evangelical pietism of his youth, in which the generation of his great-grandfather migrated to Missouri to escape religious quarrels and to embrace an ecumenical, irenic, and pietist spirit. The tradition he grew up within also resisted closure and was one reason the catechism that he memorized at thirteen had very little interpretation. It was mostly just Scripture. This was the same reason that his people accepted the little Lutheran Confession, the Augsburg Confession, and the Westminster

Catechism. Walter found in Jewish theology a seed of freedom from his childhood, a seed that had long lain somewhat dormant in the soil of his soul. He grew up surrounded by a theology of grace but had completely missed the experience of grace and of doing and being good enough. The implication of both Jewish thought and that of Evangelical Pietism is that we have not fully decoded or domesticated God nor God's text. Nor shall we ever. For Walter, the holiness or "otherness" of God is a much more elemental category than the love of God or the mercy of God or the faithfulness of God. There is always more light to bring forth from God's word. Always more revelation. Always more openness. Always more freedom. An exercise that Brueggemann sometimes did in the classroom was to imagine, as he and his students exegeted the passage of the day, that this was the only part of the biblical text that they had access to and, this being the case, would it be enough? One must suspect that Walter believes so.

All of Walter's pivots have some element of the prophetic imagination within them. He had borrowed the idea of imagination from philosopher Paul Ricoeur. Ricoeur believed that imagination was the seeing of an alternative reality to the one that lies in front of us. Brueggemann applied that idea to the biblical text and the God of that text to show that the primary work of the prophet was to see by faith God's alternative. Human beings rarely see beyond what is in front of them. The entire narrative of Scripture points toward faith as the capacity to see beyond what is. St. Paul might as well have written that "without 'prophetic imagination' it is impossible to please God!" The entire lineup of Hebrews 11 is composed of saints who saw an alternative and were seekers of that "better city." The role of the prophet is to cast a vision of that alternative reality. In his own life of the mind and heart, Walter was able to see alternatives to moralism, to the abandonment of the biblical text, to categories that closed the book on God so that God may as well have been dead. Walter saw alternatives for students who had never thought seriously about being either pastors or theologians. He saw alternatives for a curriculum that needed to be recentered in the biblical text. He saw alternative realities for the chaos and crises of the 1960s and 1970s. And he saw alternatives for his own life that slowly moved him, pivot by pivot toward freedom.

It was in Chicago, in May 2002, that the capacity of this prophet to articulate an alternative reality for Marc Nelesen saved Marc's life. One suspects there are many lives saved by this prophet who just kept drilling, drilling, and drilling the same method of reading Scripture. Why? So that the rest of us might come to understand that seeing this alternative reality for ourselves is not voodoo or science or magic. But that all of us who live within the biblical narrative, and give that narrative and its God free rein, just might at the intersection of darkness and light, like Marc Nelesen, choose the Light. For this reason, Walter Brueggemann will always be part of *Marc's narrative*.

But so few of us take the time to allow the text to lead us toward prophetic imagination. Why?

> We want a clear line of reasoning that leads to a conclusion. And the text will not cooperate. The text always involves us in ambiguity and uncertainty and openness. We want assurances. Living with that playful uncertainty in the text, I think, is more than most people want to give to it. It is probably too

grandiose. But you cannot move to a critical understanding of the Bible if you don't
move to a critical understanding of yourself.
Psychological work must go on at the same
time. The church has tried to bring people
to a critical reading of the Bible but without any of the work of the self. That must go
along with it. And that is present in the text.[3]

FIVE

No Text–No God

*It's the embarrassing things about the Bible that give
it the juice!*

Walter Brueggemann

Reverend Clover Reuter Beal dreaded the knock on the door that she knew was coming. A late evening email from a frustrated parishioner was just the thing she did not need before drifting off to sleep. Why had she bothered to look at her phone one more time before going to bed? She was relatively new to this congregation and felt the urgency to pay attention to concerns and questions that members had about her ministry. Clover had grown up in a Pentecostal congregation. So how had she ended up Presbyterian? And the pastor at that? So much of her spiritual DNA was still hard-wired to the experiences of church in her childhood. The free expressions of praise. Raising hands in worship. Spontaneous testimonies of "God-sightings" and inexplicable healings of all sorts of diseases. Outbursts of "God is good! All the time!" And then there were the prophetic words. Members could stand and freely share something God had spoken to them that week. That the second coming of Jesus was imminent. That Aunt Martha had seen an angel on her deathbed. That the pastor's last sermon was not a word from the Lord. That the candidate running for governor was anointed by God.

Church was cosmic drama. The sense of the "Lord's presence" could be felt. The Bible was real and to be taken literally. But God also spoke to individuals directly. Were these special words equivalent to Scripture? No one ever asked. But everyone was sure that their word aligned with the Scripture. Clover often wondered about that. It was clear what it meant to be a Christian, and that if one stayed within the parameters of the narrow way, heaven was assured. Periodically someone would speak in tongues, though it was never obvious when or why or for what. But emotion, affect, and feelings were all part of the religious experience of Clover's upbringing. And though much had changed about her understanding of God and the biblical text, she remained deeply connected to the "heart religion" of her childhood, to the belief that the Bible was God's Word, that God was moved by prayer, and that the community of faith was still the place where the Story was most easily accessed.

FOLLOWING BRUEGGEMANN

So how in the world had she ended up a Presbyterian—often considered the far opposite of her own upbringing and religious DNA? And how had she and her partner Tim, who also grew up an evangelical, ended up moving in the same direction together? The answer—other than Providence—was Professor Walter Brueggemann. Clover and Tim were both undergraduates at Seattle Pacific University in the mid-1980s. Both were interested not only in each other, but in continuing their education in the study of religion, Bible, and theology. Though Seattle Pacific was within the evangelical tradition, one of their faculty mentors strongly encouraged them to study with Professor Brueggemann: "Go wherever he goes!" Whether this was the word of the Lord or not, they never did decide at the time. But looking back, the answer is clear. They began to investigate Professor Brueggemann's whereabouts and why it was so imperative that they follow him like Abraham and Sarah followed YHWH and Ruth followed Naomi. They discovered that, in fact, Brueggemann was also on the move. After a quarter-century at Eden Seminary, he was packing his bags too. Whether it was because the Spirit was calling or because the current president was so recalcitrant no one knew for sure. But God moves in mysterious ways and in the divine mystery of it all the three of them ended up at Columbia Theological Seminary at just about the same time.

Of course, the reception that Professor Brueggemann received was quite different from the Beals. Walter was a rising star. Along with Brevard Childs of Yale, he would soon be considered one of the two leading Old Testament theologians in the United States. He was given the perks he finally deserved for all that he had accomplished—a secretary, a schedule amendable to writing, financial support, and an esteemed group of colleagues. In many ways, Brueggemann's presence completed the dream team that Columbia Seminary was aiming to create. Walter had been invited to teach at Columbia previously, and like every other invitation turned it down. But now he was here!

Clover and Tim, on the other hand, settled into their new lives as most graduate students are known to do. Small apartment. Budget meals. Trying to make connections. Nervous and anxious about starting all

over again. At least they had each other. They had
been warned by other students that Brueggemann was
incredibly smart, often dramatic, and sometimes a bit
of a curmudgeon. He called on anybody and everybody. He expected the reading to be done and notes
taken. He danced around the classroom, gesticulating
wildly at times, and dropping the F-bomb in the middle of a deep conversation about God. He was never
abusive or intentionally demeaning. He was just damn
excited about the biblical text. And if for a moment he
thought you were not, he had ways of making it clear
that two choices lay ahead. Get with the program or
go home! Few would ever choose the latter, regardless
of their interest in the Bible. Because what came out of
this man's mouth was mystery and awe and power and
energy and light and promise and hope that came from
another world. It was as if he could see beyond where
they were in that classroom, into an alternative reality that took them all back to 587 BCE and the nation
of Israel. If Brueggemann was Jeremiah—which was
clear—then who were they going to be? False prophet
peers of Jeremiah who claimed that what lay in front of
them was real and true? One of the church bureaucrats
who was worried more about next year's budget than
about Jeremiah's predictions of an imminent invasion
by Babylon? Were they going to be like King Hezekiah
who, hearing the bad news, replied, "At least it won't
happen in my lifetime" (Hezekiah 38:1–5)? Or like
King Jehoiakim, who took Jeremiah's words and threw
them in the fire (Jeremiah 36)? Or like poor Baruch,
Jeremiah's scribe, who was tasked with rewriting the
entire thing all over again? It was lucky for everyone
that Baruch was known for paying attention. No one
had listened more deeply to the fire in Jeremiah's bones
than his loyal friend Baruch.

IT'S ABOUT THE TEXT

In all the drama and swinging arms and gesticulation, Professor Brueggemann was forcing upon each student the question: "What are you going to do with this text?" Not what is your neighbor doing with it? Or your mother and father, or even your pastor. But what are you, prospective preacher and teacher of this text going to do with it? The choices were abundant but really came down to three in Brueggemann's mind. Join the liberals and the historical-critical scholarship that believed the words of the text to be inert and powerless and the God of that text deceased. If that was your choice, then get the hell out of seminary and go save the whales! Or join the conservatives who'd already decided, in the nineteenth century, what the text and the God of the text were up to. By doing so they had created closure to the text, inserted their own interpretations into it, codified it in their own language, and created a God in their image of themselves. If that was your choice, again get the hell out and go to Sunday School.

What Brueggemann presented was something far different. An alternative that neither Clover nor Tim had confronted in their churches or as undergraduates. But while different, there were echoes of their past that whispered to them from Brueggemann's blackboard and all the wild and woolly antics he performed. It sounded like holiness. Like mystery. Like a spring. Sounds like they had not heard for some time. Sounds that had gotten covered up with a lot of other noise—much of it from the church. The first time Clover heard Walter preach in the seminary chapel it felt as if tongues of fire rose from the top of his head. He was preaching from the book of Isaiah. She could feel the presence of God in his aliveness. She remembers weeping. Tim and Clover began to understand why they had come to Columbia. They thought they came to find Walter, and they did. But more than that, they found God again and, in some ways, for the first time.

WHO IS THIS GOD?

Professor Brueggemann portrayed a God who was free. Who could not be bound by socially constructed realities. Who lived above humanity but at the same time had come to dwell with humanity. A God who could change God's mind, meaning that the prayers of the saints mattered. Clover had always struggled with that. If God never changes, then why pray? If God has decided in advance, then why ask? Until Walter, no one could give her a straight answer. And if God was freed, so was the Word of God. One couldn't put closure around the Bible, which is why it came alive whenever one went back to the same text again and again. Tim and Clover learned that God was in recovery from God's self, and that this explained the violence of God in the Old Testament and the Word made flesh in the new. They heard that there is no God outside this text— quite a contrary perspective to the free-flowing spontaneous words of Clover's Pentecostal congregation. They learned that Freud and Marx had something to teach the church. They began to comprehend a God that felt vaguely familiar but also wildly and freely different from everything they had heard in Sunday School. And like so many others drawn to Brueggemann, it was this combination of familiar orthodoxy and unfamiliar "otherness" of God that kept them connected to Walter. He was neither progressive nor conservative. He neither rejected God nor did he accept the God imposed upon the Bible by so many others. He was a lover of the church but a loyal critic as well. He was, it seemed, an equal opportunity opponent of all poles and extremes. His sermons usually included something to offend just about everybody. Probably even himself.

PROBLEMS ON BOTH SIDES

Progressives seemed to receive Walter more readily, even making him a kind of renegade leader of their team, promoting peace and social justice, civil rights, and gay rights, and fighting racism. And indeed, he was on their team. But what they missed was that Walter believed God was the leader of their team and he was going where God was. He believed ever increasingly that God was on the side of the poor, marginalized, downtrodden, betrayed, and abused. And if one wanted to be on God's side, you better get on theirs. Find them—find God. And the other way around. Decades later, Walter regrets that some of the progressives who constituted his habitat were not sufficiently attentive to the deep claims he made for God. Over time he felt betrayed by progressives who had betrayed God. He felt deceived by those who had given up sound doctrine. He had begun his career rooted in the irenic and ecumenical posture of the Evangelical Synod of North America. Coming out of the religious wars of Europe, their mantra was "love God and neighbor." Be magnanimous, for quarrels will only destroy and divide. And give wide latitude to theological differences while being charitable in all things.

But too many progressives loved his social ethic while ignoring his grounding of this ethic in the biblical text. And few ever understood the rich German evangelical pietism out of which Brueggemann consistently responded. Evangelicals were repulsed by his early support for the ordination of gays and his affirmation of egalitarianism among men and women in church leadership. They dismissed or failed to see his high regard for the Bible and that social justice concerns emerged from his understanding of God and God's Word. The one thing that both progressives and conservatives missed was the one thing that Walter cared about the most—the text and its God.

Curiously, it was Pentecostals like Clover who, among evangelicals, warmly accepted Walter and most seemed to understand him. In 1996 he was invited by Rickie Moore to present a paper at the annual meeting of the Society for Pentecostal Studies. The society had organized a homage to Walter for his work. He was warmly received and adored for his high view of the Bible. For some reason, they cared less than other evangelicals that he bent toward Marx and appeared liberal on social issues. At least he dared to state his love for the Bible. Agree or not with the man's understanding of where the text took him, at least he stayed in the text on his journey there. It was hard for anyone who took the time to listen to miss the fact that he loved the Bible, grounded himself there daily, and was saturated with the holy.

Brueggemann was always hard to nail down theologically. But this reflected the way he also saw God and the biblical text. He liked to say that "it's hard to get God said right!" And so perhaps it wasn't that he intentionally played hard to get as much as his zig-zagging and pivoting here and there was simply his version of big game hunting. The progressives said there was no big game anymore, and evangelicals assumed they had tamed all the remaining big game. Progressives indeed seemed to receive Walter more readily and assumed he was on their team. And indeed, he was. But they missed that Walter believed that God was on their team and he was going where God was. He believed that God was on the side of the poor, marginalized, downtrodden, betrayed, and abused. And if one wanted to be on God's side, you better get on theirs. Find them—find God. But also the other way around.

Decades later, Walter has some regret that progressives in the church composed his habitat. Over time he felt betrayed by progressives who had betrayed God. They loved his social ethic while ignoring his grounding of this ethic in the biblical text. Evangelicals were so repulsed by his early support for the ordination of gays and his affirmation of egalitarianism among men and women in church leadership. They missed his high regard for the Bible and his understanding that social justice concerns emerged from his understanding of God and God's Word. The one thing that both missed was the one thing that Walter cared about the most.

Then Clover heard a knock at the door. It was the disturbed parishioner. He had heard of Clover's efforts to develop a back-to-the-Bible educational program for adults. Clover invited him to sit down. He blurted out, "I hear the Adult Faith Formation team is focusing on the Bible this year. I am uneasy with the Bible and many in this highly educated church are as well. Some have Bible baggage from their upbringing; some have no understanding of the text at all." Clover replied, "Professor Walter Brueggemann did recommend me for this position, and here is why." From there on the conversation was easy for Clover. She shared what she had learned of his convictions about the Bible. His high view of Scripture allowed the text to speak. She paused as the parishioner let this sink in. He warmed to Clover as he heard her describe the multilayered mysteries of

the text and the openness of the text to ongoing interrogation and revelation. The God who lived in that text
could not be confined by the human constructs of the
text. "Dr. Brueggemann has shaped generations of pastors and preachers and scholars. I feel like I try to wear
his mantle to continually challenge the church to take
seriously the biblical text and its rich stories. We need to
do the Bible and ask what it is doing to us. We need to
be people of the text."

She continued, "God is in covenant, which means
God is in the risky business of being willing to be
affected by us. God holds up God's end of the deal.
Prayer is a way of getting at our deepest desires of being
in relationship with God and being in relationship in
and with the world. It's an intimate relationship. How
do we know that biblical God, other than in the stories of the Bible? These are the stories we have. How
about you join us next week for a reading circle of about
thirty-five people?" He paused. "Thank you for introducing me more closely to Brueggemann." She escorted
the man to the door and went back to her computer.
First, she paused and thanked God for rich conversations such as those. Then she sent a quick note of thanks
to Walter for continuing to shape her and draw her into
a greater engagement with the Bible.

BRUEGGEMANN'S GOD

Throughout Brueggemann's life, his understanding of
God has matured in conversation with numerous conversation partners—some dead and some living. Our
social worlds were constructed by others long before our
births. We grow up in those worlds and assign names to
people, places, and things. During our early formation

those people, places, and things become ours. We carry them with us. We take them for granted. We are produced by and products of our worlds. And many of us are relatively content to remain as we are and with our world as it is. But now and then someone dares to confront, challenge, and criticize that world. Someone who does not assume that what is seen is all that there is. Someone who does not believe that the package of goods they purchased is the only package available. And if they have the courage and stamina and imagination, they will lead us into new realities that they can see when no one else can. And in this way we construct or produce new worlds. These worlds are not totally disconnected from the Old World. They are not as comfortable as in the Old World. But they have the chance to relocate what was best about the old while pointing to a future we are likely never to see. These folks are producers of new worlds.

The genius of Walter Brueggemann lies in his life-long assault on the taken-for-granted realities of the church, the world, his life, the academy, and the biblical text and that text's God. He has never been willing to say "I have learned enough. I have seen enough. I have done enough. Now let your servant depart in peace." Brueggemann never created closure for the biblical text but constantly assumes that it will reveal something new and different every time he lays his eyes on it. And he has always done so in conversation with others, understanding that our social worlds are constructed and sustained as we do so. We never make durable worlds alone, but always in conversation with others. The degree with which Brueggemann has articulated one new insight after another about the text and its God is wholly dependent upon his ongoing conversation partners who have challenged, confronted, and affirmed. While having few mentors he has had many partners, and these partners have impacted the insights he has produced.

BEYOND A GOD OF MIGHTY DEEDS

The reigning paradigm in Old Testament theology as Walter came of age was historical form criticism. Julius Wellhausen and Hermann Gunkel were the fathers of these modes of critical study that continued to mature through the work of Martin Noth and Gerhard von Rad. But after Wellhausen, Gunkel had already allowed for an aesthetic sensibility alongside the dominance of rationalism. It is this aesthetic sensibility that was available to Brueggemann as mediated to him, especially through Allen Wehrli and James Muilenburg.

Gerhard von Rad held an academic position in Germany following the fall of the Third Reich. A pastor in the Confessing Church that resisted Hitler, von Rad broke ranks with his peers in moving beyond historical form criticism toward an interpretive mode that spoke to the church. His was a separate stream from that of Muilenburg, but both impacted Brueggemann. Form criticism was concerned with the genre of a particular text. Literate patterns were important. The historical context was everything. It was German rationality at its best applied to the Bible—counting, classifying, containing, and controlling. Scholars focused on the mighty deeds of God in history but offered little space for the deeds of a mighty God today. The text remained flat, inert, and ultimately meaningless.

Brueggemann had trained in this mode at Eden Seminary and to some degree at Union also. But it was James Muilenburg leading the charge against historical criticism who had the greatest impact on Walter's direction. Walter relied upon the foundation of form criticism to locate a text in history and to understand its historical context. But while form-critical scholars stopped there and laid down their pipes, Walter was just lighting up. There were rhetorical connections yet to make. There was a sociological interpretation to add. And then there were the most important questions: What in God's name is happening in the text? Is God absent or present? Abusive or merciful? Violent or peacemaking? Making an end of God's people or not? And then what does all of this mean for God's people today? What is the application to the civil rights movement and the continued oppression of Black Americans? To gay and lesbian followers of Jesus? To 9/11 and the war in Iraq? To a president who wants to "make America great again?" No wonder Brueggemann loved what he did. No wonder pastors were ignited by the fire that burned in his bones. No wonder students who never thought about it before decided to become theologians. No wonder Clover's parishioner warmed to her altar call, all the while channeling Walter. While the endgame for historical criticism was itself the end, Walter's approach was ever-changing and the means to an end that never fully reveals itself. He understood that the text has a proclamation and the job of the interpreter is to grow sensitive to it, and then be able to know to translate it into the current time.

A FRIEND'S SCATHING CRITIQUE

The audience had gathered to honor the outstanding contributions of Professor Walter Brueggemann to the scholarly guild. The focus was on his highly touted and recently published magisterial *Theology of the Old Testament*. An international collection of scholars delivered papers timed to celebrate his sixty-fifth birthday: Gottwald, Trible, Gunn, O'Connor, Miller, Westermann, Fretheim, and more. Most of his colleagues offered laudatory words that affirmed some aspect of this significant volume and his work in general. It would not have been the academy if he had not received some pushback, challenges to revisit some element of his thinking, and critiques of this or that interpretation of the text.

But it is likely that no one, including Walter, was prepared for the relentless and critical assessment of his friend and longest-running conversation partner, Professor Terry Fretheim of Luther Seminary. Fretheim was scathing in his critique.[1] But he moved beyond Walter's work to a blunt assessment of the man himself. Fretheim began by acknowledging the challenge of getting a grasp on Walter's theology because of his nonstop publishing and changing perspectives. Fretheim has concerns with the ambivalence and ambiguity of Walter's God. He was unsettled by the unsettled interior life that Brueggemann attributes to God. He critiqued Walter's belief that there is "no God outside the text." He finds his colleague inconsistent in rejecting methods and assumptions that he then turns around and employs. He struggles with the way that, when backed into a corner, Brueggemann tends to fall back on a Calvinist-like commitment to God's sovereignty. He renounces his friend's acceptance that the rhetoric about God by God's people represents who God is. He believes that Walter stays too confined to rhetoric and does not engage history and ontology sufficiently. Brueggemann's theology too readily minimizes grace and God's love for a broken world. If God is so hard to nail down, then he becomes the most frightening of beings, whose unpredictability can be used by anyone to legitimize their personal claims. He gives priority to God's sovereignty while downplaying God's faithfulness. He supports a violent and abusive God. He labels God with inaccurate and irreligious qualities not found in the Scripture. For one who says that he stays in the text, he sure has a curious way of moving out of it when he wants to. It was difficult that evening to hear much if any affirmation of the monumental effort that his friend's *Theology of the Old Testament* made to scholarship. He ends by acknowledging Brueggemann's contribution as a challenge to the adequacy of core confessions.

The two had a long history of conversation around the themes of the sovereignty and faithfulness of God. Fretheim came down on the side of faithfulness—God consistently illustrated God's provision and care and grace. God was constrained by God's promises of faithfulness. God's fidelity demanded that God carry out the promises. If one subverted faithfulness to sovereignty, one opens the doors to a potentially abusive and violent God who is scarier than hell.

WHY OUR ORIGINS AND SOCIALIZATION MATTER

Fretheim would pass away in 2020, another one of Walter's peers to meet their Maker before him. As is typical in his responses to those who disagreed with him, he found a way to eulogize the best of Fretheim. He called Terry a great friend, a great force, a great teacher, and a greater pastor. He credited Fretheim as the leader of their discipline for the last fifteen years. He noted that both came out of the best of German pietism. He suggested that Fretheim saw him within a strong Calvinist mold coming out of the Prussian Union. This meant that Walter leaned too much on God's sovereignty and thus God as an agent and primary actor to intervene in the world. Brueggemann, however, saw Fretheim as giving away too much of God's agency. Walter, characteristically, moved away from quarreling with his friend and claimed the high road after it was too late for Terry to respond. He simply noted that their differences were likely related to their theological socializations, personalities, and social positions. And he made an effort to attend Fretheim's memorial service and spoke at the service.[2]

In the end, this scholarly debate between Fretheim and Brueggemann, and their corresponding responses to the other, was indeed consistent with the theological traditions from which each emerged. They were nearly the same age and both of their fathers were pastors, but beyond that the historical and biographical differences are substantial. While Walter emerged from the Prussian Union tradition, Fretheim came from the Norwegian Lutheran tradition. His great-grandfather, Erick, migrated as a farmer from Norway to Minnesota. Fretheim's grandfather Erick graduated from Luther Seminary as did his father, Earling. Both father and grandfather were well trained, consistent with the Lutheran emphasis on scholarship and education. His great-uncle was also a Lutheran pastor and officiated at his great-grandfather and great-grandmother's "pretty" wedding. The tradition of pastor families was strong in the Norwegian Lutheran tradition. Children of pastors were well-positioned socioeconomically. Terry's grandfather Erick was born just a few years apart from Walter's father. Walter's grandfather Wilhelm was a German immigrant and irreligious freethinker. His father August was a farmer turned pastor who barely slipped through seminary. Walter was a second-generation American, and Terry of the third. Terry was the oldest child of his family and Walter the youngest. Brueggemann and Fretheim met with each coming out of very different socially constructed worlds that they had internalized. And while both went beyond those worlds to some degree, each carried with them the religious and cultural DNA of their childhoods.

The socioeconomic differences between the two could not have been starker. Walter always felt behind due to his humble beginnings. Terry had little reason to feel the same. Walter came from a church tradition where pastors were marginalized, treated poorly, paid little, and always expected to be available. Terry came from a Scandinavian Lutheran tradition where pastors had high social standing and were much better paid. Walter knew nothing of higher education and graduate training as a teenager. Terry grew up steeped in that culture for generations. Walter felt insecure for decades about his position relative to those in Ivy League academic institutions. Terry interacted freely with folks from these places and went to Princeton. The surprise in these two stories is not that Terry ended up a scholar of esteem, but that Walter did so. Walter's eulogy reflects his understanding that a deeper exegesis of each of their lives would likely shed light on why they differed theologically, and how they read and interpreted the text. And yet in it he also wonders whether their conversations about differences included the interrogation of the other's socially constructed world. Did they recognize how their backgrounds impacted the way they approached the biblical text and the conclusions they made? The magnanimous approach that Walter took to his critics, including Terry, reflected his grounding in the pietism of his fathers and mothers. For all their disagreement, in the end, the two shared a deep and joyous affirmation of the commanding claims of Scripture. It was an honest, glad friendship.

Fretheim and many Lutheran scholars were suspicious of German pietism and tended to write off the Lutheran dimension of the Prussian Union as less than truly Lutheran. Thus, he saw Walter within the Calvinist camp and pegged him as falling back on God's sovereignty. Conversely Walter recognized Terry's appreciation of Lutheran pietism that had emerged in Germany as a reaction to the high Scholasticism of Lutheranism. Walter's people of the Prussian Union were skeptical of the impact of the Enlightenment upon faith and religion. Scandinavian Lutherans were less concerned. Both Walter and Terry were grinding the axes of their traditions. And they were often grinding together. As conversation partners, their mutual grinding undoubtedly complemented one another more than they were aware of at the time. Walter was a poet more than anything else. He took the Bible seriously but not literally. The academy was just one more location among many where God had led him to speak a provocative prophetic word. He had come to terms with the fact that his primary work was for the church. Pastors like Clover accepted the ambivalence and ambiguity that Walter brought perhaps because their worlds as pastors were in the real world that was so messy, disoriented, and in disequilibrium. His students embraced his message in large part because he was so excited about learning and about God. This was all so new to them as students trained in the rational educational industrial complex of the United States. Walter's approach was free, unconstrained, and far removed from anything that they had experienced academically.

But it was in the academy where Brueggemann faced his greatest challenges, skepticism, and critique. Being so broadly read and so committed to interdisciplinary discovery, he spoke in the language and jargon of other disciplines that many of his peers were familiar with. For the same reason, he spoke from theoretical perspectives they were unfamiliar with. He intentionally positioned himself outside the specializations of the academy. By doing so he moved across sacred parameters where specialists were likely to get him in their sights and nail him on specifics that were secondary to Walter's primary message about the text. His curiosity drove him across these interdisciplinary lines. His refusal to be siloed within one specialization also resulted in his being able to communicate with ordinary pastors and their ordinary pew-dwellers. Brueggemann never forgot that language is how we make our worlds; and an academy that forgets the language of the church no longer contributes to the church. This was the reason for his resistance to the historical-critical model and he had cautioned the SBL of the same during his 1990 presidential address.

While scholars may choose to stay in the weeds debating the language of a poet—a hopeless cause altogether but one that keeps granting tenure and promotion—pastors like Clover Reuter Beal and Mark Nelesen live on the edge of their seats to gain every word. Tim Beal and Tod Linafelt, editors of the Brueggemann Festschrift and former students of Walter's, seem to understand the poetic quality of their mentor by beginning their Introduction to the book with a quote from poet William Blake:

> The prophets Isaiah and Ezekiel dined with
> me, and I asked them how they dared so
> roundly to assert that God spake to them;

and whether they did not think at the time, that they would be misunderstood, and so be the cause of imposition. Isaiah answered. I saw no God nor heard any . . . as I was then persuaded and remained confirmed; that the voice of honest indignation is the voice of God, I cared not for the consequences I wrote. Then I asked: does a firm persuasion that a thing is so, make it so? He replied. All poets believe that it does, and in the ages of imagination this firm persuasion removed mountains, but many are not capable of a firm persuasion of anything. I heard this with some wonder, and must confess my own conviction.[3]

While scholars and not pastors, Beal and Linafelt sat under Brueggemann's spell at Columbia Seminary. They were scared speechless on the first day of their course on the Pentateuch because of Brueggemann's reputation. But fear turned to awe at his magic, his alchemy, his saturation in the holy. Like Clover, they too had drunk the Kool-Aid and found that it quenched a lifelong thirst to be brought into the presence of the Almighty and the Almighty's sanctuary. And though in the academy, their critiques of their professor and mentor are those of deeply loved students who deeply love this prophet-poet. While academic analysis tends to squelch or kill the beauty of a thing, poetry always brings it back to life. And perhaps one's reaction to Brueggemann's work comes down to one's openness to the self-disclosure and acceptance of ambivalence and ambiguity that every poet carries. The capacity to live at the intersection of light and darkness and freedom and moralism just might be the key as to whether one is drawn toward Brueggemann's work or repelled from it.

ALWAYS MENTORING

Kathleen O'Connor heard the phone ring. It was Louis Stulman. He was calling unexpectedly to suggest that the two of them begin a section on the study of Jeremiah at the SBL meeting that year. Kathleen was a graduate of Princeton in Old Testament Studies and Louis from Drew University. They shared an interest in the study of Jeremiah but had never thrown around the idea of starting a session on Jeremiah at the annual meetings of the SBL. Louis told Kathleen that he was ready to write up a formal proposal. She was delighted and the two worked to plan the first year's paper presentations at the SBL annual meeting in 1990 in New Orleans—the same year as Brueggemann's presidential address.

Kathleen was particularly delighted to be engaged in this kind of scholarly activity, given that she had not exactly landed in the most traditional of academic positions following Princeton. She had since 1982 taught at the Maryknoll School of Theology. As a Roman Catholic, her fit at this Catholic institution that prepared individuals to serve abroad was life-altering. The nature of her teaching assignments was for seminary and lay students preparing to serve and translate the Gospel abroad, largely in places of poverty and oppression. Her approach could not be the same educational approach that she experienced at Princeton. There, the dominant approach to studying the Old Testament was a historical-critical mode that offered little to those preparing for ministry, especially in Africa, Asia, and Latin America.

Kathleen had only encountered Brueggemann through *The Prophetic Imagination,* which she often used in class. She found herself having to translate many academic analytical studies for a community of people who were working out there among these global citizens. The principal scholar she could find to help her was Walter Brueggemann, whose prophetic imagination offered hope for the desperation, pain, oppression, and trauma of both her students and those she was preparing them to minister to.

Kathleen's first personal exchange with Walter was at a reception, at the Society of Biblical Literature gathering in 1990. It was at the reception following Brueggemann's presidential address in which he had just preached a sermon to the SBL crowd, cautioning them against being the first generation of scholars who failed to pass on the sacred text to the next generation. Kathleen reached out to Walter, telling him that she loved his review of the three Jeremiah commentaries that he had published in 1988. She thanked him for his line that the "church deserved better." Her affirmation came at just the right time for Brueggemann, who at about that very moment was taking heat from one of those three commentary authors. She shared her work with Walter and, in the coming years, connected at professional conferences. In 1995 Kathleen was called to Columbia Seminary, where for the next decade she would be the colleague of one whom she had so admired years earlier and whose work brought life to her teaching and her students. Kathleen would come to disagree in some direct ways with Walter's interpretation of the violence and abusive nature of God. The two of them had many conversations about their differences, and she found him to be one to whom you could not close your ears or your eyes, and very often you couldn't turn your heart against him. He just was so profoundly effective.

Louis Stulman first encountered Brueggemann's work as a graduate student at Drew University. Picking up one of Brueggemann's early books on Hosea off his Old Testament professor's desk, Louis was immediately struck by his rigorous exegetical analysis that moved readily into praxis and contemporaneity. Louis would later look back and realize that this interpretive perspective was simply vintage Walter. Years later when teaching seminary and university students in Findlay, Ohio, Louis met Walter for the first time at an SBL conference with Louis informing Walter that he was one of three persons whose writings had most profoundly influenced him—the others being Abraham Heschel and Henri Nouwen. Walter responded, "that's tough company to be a part of."

Thus, began a working relationship with Walter and eventually Kathleen O'Connor and Pete Diamond. They invited Ronald Clements, Walter Brueggemann, Robert Carroll, and William Holladay to join the steering committee of the SBL Jeremiah consultation and course to speak at the sessions, all powerhouses in the study of Jeremiah by this point. The three young scholars felt dwarfed by these giants, but, at the same time, they were breaking ground on approaches to the book that moved beyond conventional historical readings. This research within the Jeremiah section was developing amid the massive paradigm shift from historical-critical analysis to the kind of rhetorical analysis that Walter had long been pioneering. And so, these younger scholars found in Walter a willing collaborator and mentor. He was extraordinarily generous, supportive, and humble, as well as brilliant and inspiring. New life had come to a discipline that for a century had been losing its place.

In the meantime, Louis began to draw upon Walter's method and approach in his seminary and university classes on the Hebrew Bible. He introduced students to a God of the Torah liberating marginalized peoples and overthrowing neighborhood bullies—the oppressor pharaohs. This was a God of the Prophets refusing to be captive to provincial Enlightenment categories. A God of Israel's hymnal lingering in pain, no less hope. And for many in his classes, Brueggemann's groupings of orientation, disorientation, and reorientation transformed their understanding of the Psalter, providing a fresh appreciation and love for the church's prayer book. Louis found both conservative and progressive students enthusiastically embracing Brueggemann's exegetical dexterity, theological buoyancy, and refusal to imprison the text in the past, along with a dynamic pietism and spirituality. And always a focus on society, ministry, and scholarship. The man was so multilayered and lived at the intersection of so many counterparts, and it was this capacity to hold ambiguity and ambivalence that made him so different from everyone else. Other scholars sought answers; Walter sought more questions. Others sought closure; Walter sought more openness. Others have more clarity; Walter more ambiguity.

Walter was such a contrast from his peers. No one dozed during his academic paper presentations. His papers were groundbreaking, imaginative, artful, and dramatic. They were sermons. While twenty or maybe thirty people might show up to most paper sessions, one couldn't find a seat when Walter spoke. Sometimes hundreds crowded into the halls. Many scheduled their conference agenda around his presentations. He was once-in-a-generation kind of figure. His presence had made it possible for papers to be presented that would not have gotten a hearing before Brueggemann. Papers that included God. Papers for the church.

THE TIPPING POINT

Perhaps the tipping point in the struggle for the soul of Old Testament studies would come in 1988 when three commentaries on Jeremiah were published, all by well-known peers of Walter. Walter wrote an essay entitled "Jeremiah: Intense Criticism/Thin Interpretation."[4] It was a "Brueggemannish" title that made the direction of his essay clear as soon as he left the starting gate. Brueggemann assesses the three most recent Jeremiah commentaries. He has little to commend in any of them. While they differ in degree, they continue to reflect what he has spent his calling trying to bury. Like gophers, the heads of the historical critics keep finding enough energy to make one more appearance. The advantage of three coming out at once was that Brueggemann only needed one mallet and one fell swoop to at least throw them off-balance. It was as if Brueggemann understood the stakes if he failed to deftly but with strength and courage outrun the dying horse of historical criticism which had found a way to hang on for so damn long. But this was Walter's hour, and in just two years he would be elected president of the SBL. As one who coveted this role, he had to know that this particularly scathing critique of giants in his field was no way to run a successful campaign. But Walter knew what he was up against and he would remain vintage Walter.

He critiqued the three commentaries for continuing to play out of the old and tired historical-critical mode. He describes Holladay as being "embarrassingly specific" in his rational approach to counting and classifying within the text.[5] He is slightly more positive about Carroll's commentary; in the end, it represents just more of the same "long-standing historical focus." The commentary by McKane is, as expected, "loaded with textual detail in the most ponderous way" and "exceedingly hard going." It is "nearly unreadable" unless one is a specialist in this kind of technical work. In four short pages Brueggemann made short shrift of these homogeneous examples of "what critical scholarship can do and do well." The problem with doing well, which is no longer meaningful and relevant to the church, means that these three authors have wasted an awful lot of their time. They were smart enough to read between the lines.

But Brueggemann lingers not and launches into the question of what a good commentary should do. At that moment he appeals to the work of the one person he identifies as a mentor to him—Bernhard Anderson of Princeton. It may have been that he genuinely wanted to express Anderson's views, but it is also possible that the mentor who had modeled courage for Walter before the academy was showing up to again remind Walter to be courageous and to remember the stakes of the eternal race. Not only had Walter watched Anderson be courageous, but he had also heard him challenge Walter to let go of what others might say or do in response. Know it or not, Anderson was nurturing the shift in Walter's long journey from moralism to freedom. Anderson shared Walter's concerns that one's focus must be on both the academy and the church. He believed one should step into contemporary hermeneutical debates and "take a firm stand."

With a senior scholar like Anderson pulling Walter forward and the bevy of young enthusiastic scholars pushing against him from behind, Brueggemann concludes with deep conviction:

If we grant even the most general claim of the text that this is a live authorizing word that continues to have the power to liberate imagination for obedience and daring, then we are bound to ask what the text continues to say that matters, how we listen with availability, and how in our interpretation the continued saying and the available listening are brought together. . . . How could it be that the text of Jeremiah might describe our human life to permit new perceptions, new actions, new compassions, new obedience, and new hopes?[6]

The answers to his own questions smell of the German evangelical pietism of his youth. They reflect the life of one who has met the God of the text and has learned to "listen with availability" and to "ask what the text continues to say?" These were certainly not questions of the last one hundred years among most historical critics in the academy. Questions for preachers week in and week out, but hardly of scholars.

Prayers about injustice, the moral coherence that God brings to our lives, hope for exiled people, a transcendent answerability, and a God whose heart is rent by the pain God feels—while asked as questions, these had always been Walter's answers, ever since growing up in the Evangelical Synod where his people were done with religious quarrels and ready to simply "love God and neighbor" and hold a commitment to "in essentials unity, in non-essentials liberty, and in all things charity." Walter entered the academy thoroughly drenched in residue coming out of the Prussian Union and its children who came to Missouri. Walter had little time for jot and tittle. He could fillet it with the truth in short order. And once again he did so, raising the eyes of his readers to see what God was doing, what God was up to, and what in the world all of that had to do with their pain, doubt, fear, trauma, terror, and guilt?

Not only were younger scholars looking to find authentic answers from the text if it still spoke, but so was a new generation of pastors and pew-dwellers alike. When Kathleen O'Connor read this essay by Walter she jumped up and down in her living room with joy. She might have been Catholic, but this Protestant had it figured out! And when Walter showed up twice to preach at Clover Reuter Beal's church, that irritated parishioner likely did so as well.

PART THREE

PART ONE

SIX

The Secret

I am lucky—I get to spend every day in the text!
Walter Brueggemann

Reverend Roger Green had been hearing the rumors for several months: "Professor Walter Brueggemann of Columbia Seminary is moving to Cincinnati!" When he first heard the rumblings of Brueggemann's coming, he didn't think much about it. For one thing, Brueggemann was ordained in the United Churches of Christ and would probably end up at First UCC. In addition, he was leaving a Presbyterian seminary so perhaps Mt. Washington Presbyterian church would attract him. Chances were he would end up in one of those traditions. In any event, Roger had been at St. Timothy's Episcopal Church for nearly two decades. He had developed a nonanxious presence as a leader who had faced success and defeat as well as highs and lows—he could handle the renowned theologian if he had to.

He had weathered the initial growth of the congregation under his leadership. He had weathered the eventual decline as folks began to hear his messages challenging the consumer "market-driven" society (the dominant American religion) that has infected the church. He had weathered the struggles around sexuality. And he had weathered the battle to place an American flag in the sanctuary. He could certainly weather the arrival and attendance of the twentieth century's most prolific theologian. A man of Brueggemann's character was likely to be absent most Sundays anyway. Off lecturing, preaching, leading retreats, and probably taking regular, personal retreats on mountain tops to hear from God. Something had to explain the quality and quantity of his work. Undoubtedly it was connected to a deep, contemplative life. After all, that's what had gotten Roger through the low spots of ministry over the decades.

Still, he wondered what it would be like to have someone of Brueggemann's qualifications in the pews. Probably a tough critic when it came to sermons and preaching. Little did he know just how tough! Walter was known for holding his pastors to the high standard of relying upon the biblical text, exhibiting a dialogic relationship with the God of that text, and living a life that reflected a love of God and neighbor. Walter didn't think that was too much to ask. And neither would have Roger had he known. But he would find out soon enough, and he would pass Walter's assessment with flying colors.

Walter left Columbia Seminary and Decatur, Georgia, behind in 2008 following the end of his marriage to his wife Mary.[1] He moved to Cincinnati, Ohio. He married Tia. He came to slow down. To back off his workload. To be more anonymous. Maybe more autonomous too. To write and lecture less. To respond to the demands of others less. To be known less as God's prophet. He had promised his family and friends year after year that this was the last season of traveling and lecturing. He really would cut back. It had never happened but now was the chance to turn over a new leaf. He was worried about finding a church where the biblical text showed up in sermons, the pastor's eyes gleamed with passion about the text, and application of the text was made to the contemporary world. He believed in the church despite being one of its harshest critics. The church, after all, was the only carrier of the Story—even the bad ones for which he had so little time. And wherever the church was faithful, the community around the congregation was being cared for and its needs addressed. Justice and mercy showed up together. He believed in the church and he loved the church still. Despite how it had abused his father. Despite how it worshipped the empire. Despite its domestication of YHWH. Prophets don't quit on God's people because they don't quit on God.

A friend recommended that he visit St. Timothy's Episcopal Church. The pastor was known for his retaining a blazing fire in his belly for the text after nearly two decades of preaching. He was passionate about the community around the congregation and finding ways to connect with the neighborhood. The congregation stood out as one of the few in its neighborhood to make clear its commitment to social and racial justice. Roger refused to allow the congregation to be the chaplain of the American empire. Somehow, he had retained the passion and vision for mission that so often gets lost in a preacher over time. He was truly unusual.

Walter would give St. Timothy's a try. He did so, introduced himself to Roger, and they agreed to meet the following week for coffee. Little did Roger know this would be the beginning of one of the most meaningful relationships he would have at St. Timothy's. As they talked over coffee, Walter explained that he just wanted to be an ordinary church member—not to be known as Professor Walter Brueggemann. To sit in the pews; to listen to Roger preach; to participate in the

Eucharist; to sing the hymns he loved; to find fellowship with others; to embrace a new rhythm of living; to be a human being. To heal.

Over time, Walter and Reverend Green became close. Walter encouraged Roger when things became difficult in the church. He listened to Roger's anxieties. He gently offered counsel. He offered encouragement to let things die that needed to die. That death was part of the church's experience because it was the experience of its Lord. New life would come. New vision would emerge. New allies would show up. He affirmed Roger's commitment to justice and those on the margins.

When asked, he preached from time to time. Folk began to recognize who he was. He was invited to lead Bible studies. People flocked from all over the city to hear him. He responded to correspondence. He met with those who asked. He continued writing. Traveling and lecturing picked up again. And the promises and assurances that he made to others about slowing down were quickly showing themselves for what they were. Empty promises. Walter began to show signs of fatigue.

Roger decided it was time for an intervention. He invited Walter to participate in a men's contemplative prayer group. The men gathered on Saturday mornings. Walter showed up. Roger led. And then silence. Silence for meditation. Silence for contemplative prayer. And then sharing together in small groups about what God had revealed to each of them. Roger noticed that Walter seemed restless, disengaged, distracted. Roger was concerned. Surely a man of Brueggemann's stature would have some deep spiritual insight to share with the men. "Don't let me down Walter," Roger thought. But Walter remained silent. And then he departed.

"Contemplation is not really my thing," said Walter later over coffee. "You know, I try to keep up with a list of people I've promised to pray for. But my experiences with God are nearly always through the exegesis of the text." Indeed, any sense of what makes Walter who he is most readily reveals itself through his prayers, sermons, essays, and books that always begin within and from a biblical text. It's as if Walter doesn't know how to reflect except through the text. Or perhaps even think except through the text. He is immersed in the text. His father's bestowal of "The Word is a lamp unto my feet and a guide unto my way" has truly been the key to understanding what makes Walter tick. It is the secret of his life.

Like every prophet before him, he has had to keep speaking the words that God gives to him, but to speak those words he had to know those words. He had to memorize those words. He had done so at the age of thirteen during his confirmation, memorizing the Synod's catechism which was entirely grounded in the text. His dialogical relationship with God was dependent upon the text and sharing what that text said to others. Sharing how the ancient text spoke to current realities. He was not a contemplative who waited in silence; who found intercessory prayer for others easy; who had what many call personal devotions or quiet time. But he knew he was the luckiest person alive because day in and day out he saturated himself in the text. Which of course meant that he was saturated with the holy. God was not an object external to him, but God was always present with him. The way he began his prayers reflected that recognition. He rarely addressed God by name because we are always in conversation with God, and God with us. We don't move in and out of the holy but live within it.

And yet over the years, he struggled to remember that the holiness of God was not a condemning

presence but one of grace undeserved. Though he had
grown up with that message all around him, even now,
at the end of his life, he has to work to stay in that place
of grace and acceptance and that he has done enough.
After years of being motivated by shame and a sense of
inadequacy, working to acquit his sense of inferiority,
this staying in the place of grace has not been easy. For
one thing, the shame contributed to his success, productivity, and energy.

He condemned Pharaoh's intoxication with work
and achievement but struggled not to be Pharaoh's slave
himself. He preached the necessity of sabbath but found
it hard to practice himself. He so often lectured on the
fidelity of covenant but struggled to keep his end of the
bargain at times. He lamented that failure. And so, he
preached and wrote about Exodus, deliverance from
Egypt, and freedom. He wrote about the bondage of
captivity by the never-ending demands of the empire.
He studied the Psalms of lament. Poured over them.
Wrote prayers out of them. Preached out of them. Reintroduced them to the church's liturgy.

In all of this, the prophet was wrestling with his
past, his present, and with what he imagined to be
his future. He was wrestling with the divine as Jacob
wrestled with God. While always in the presence of
God, he was not always at peace with God. Like the
God whose inner being was sometimes in turmoil,
so was his. As that God lamented, so did Walter.
In some ways, everything he ever wrote and taught
and preached was his way of working out the tensions of his own soul, but he resonated with so many
because these are the shared tensions of humanity:
shame, alienation, loss, insecurity, grief. While the
text is clear that these emotions and experiences are
common fodder for lament, the church has been less

willing to believe that lament is relevant or appropriate. But Walter took lament seriously and reintroduced lament to the liturgy of the church. Arguably, he did more than anyone to return the church to lament and away from denial and false exuberance. This prophet hopes that his longest-lasting legacy will be the attention that he gave to the lament Psalms for the church.

Walter's breakthrough book, *The Prophetic Imagination*, revealed that he was a poet of the biblical text, that he stood at the intersection where so many poets stand—of light and darkness, of death and life, of freedom and moralism. And nothing he has written is more revealing of his poetry than the little-known prayers he has been writing for decades. Before class began, he would write a prayer for that day's class, based upon a text that he would be executing or based upon something that was happening in the world—some injustice, some calamity, some crisis. As he wrote he was moved; he self-disclosed; he wrestled with YHWH. He called on God to be God. To show up with power. To awaken to the injustices in the world. His prayers echoed with every theme he had ever addressed in sermons and books, but in dialogue with God. He lamented. He confessed sin. It is quite likely that more than anything he has written, he will be remembered for his prayers as they are increasingly discovered by others. For they reveal the secrets within the man and the secret strength and inspiration by which he gave utterance to the truth.

His prayers reflect his theology. Brueggemann's life teaches us that our life with God is not differentiated from our life in the Word and world. Our life with God is not simply a personal quiet time or a time of devotions or retreat, as important as those are. Our life with God is not a list of prayer requests, as important as that is. But all of these and more emerge from a deeper organic place connected to God before we were conceived. The following poem reflects Walter's turmoil as he recognizes his origins in God and his struggle to stay in that place of grace.

Mostly Glad

(On reading Psalm 139:1–18)

I always knew my life began in my home-
town, Tilden, Nebraska.
We always know our lives begin in our home
towns.
Then, later, we discover our lives began before
that,
when an egg met sperm, sometimes in
love, too often not.
Behind our hometown, an egg, and
sperm!
But then, later still, we learned, behind egg
and sperm, you!
Our life began in you.
You knit us together in your attentiveness;
You saw our skeletal structure already in
secret;
You wove our parts together;
You saw our possibility before we were
formed;
You wrote our names down in our big
Book of Life.
We are surrounded by you;
We are wrapped up in your attentiveness;
We are held in the safety of your
goodness.

Philosophers talk in a cool way of your
"omnipresence."
But there is nothing cool about you;
with you, it is over-attentiveness,
so much so that we cannot
breathe in freedom apart
from you.
We try to outrun you, but cannot;
We try to escape from you, but you are
ahead of us;
We try to outflank you or deceive you,
but your wisdom overrides our
efforts.
We find our lives God-occupied,
as though we are your primary field of
activity,
as though we are the subject of your
every thought,
as though you permeate our will and our
thought and our best resolve.
It turns out that we are not who we thought
we were . . .
detached, free, on our own, choosing our
path.
We belong to you;
sometimes that is a comfort to us;
sometimes it is a burden to us;
sometimes it is the joy of our life.
sometimes it is an embarrassment to us.
But either way—in every way—
we are yours;
we are still with you after everything,
and you are still with us.
We live our lives with reference to you.
It could not be otherwise;

mostly we do not want it otherwise;
mostly we are glad we belong to you;
mostly we are grateful and trusting,
mostly we live in glad response to
you,
mostly . . . , but not always. Amen.

Perhaps what we learn from Walter's confessional life, life with God, or whatever you call it, is that social justice is never separate from who God is or from the church and its calling. That standing for justice is part of our required witness to the world. Justice stands with God. One does not have God without justice and one does not have justice without God. This has been a message of Brueggemann's since the beginning of his writing and long before. Brueggemann grew up in a time when modernity and the rational world had not so clearly sliced and diced our lives into specialties, into categories, into boxes, where bureaucratic manifestations of rationality differentiated the church from the world and secular from spiritual and justice from witness. Modernity, which Brueggemann has resisted in his writing in all its forms, has not managed to segment Walter's life in God from his life at the grocery store, in the pulpit, in the classroom, in relationship. This wholeness in this integration of an otherwise complex human being is best expressed not in theological writings that held people in awe, but rather through his poetry and his prayers, like this poem based upon John 9.

Life Outside Our Homemade Cages

(John 9)

We live conveniently in our homemade cages
of explanation.
We live comfortably in our cages of cause
and effect.

We liberals live in our cages of being
smarter and more woke;
We conservatives live in our cages of being
better grounded and more reliable.
In our cages of ideology, we sense our control,
our ability to explain,
our capacity to link cause to effect,
to connect deed to consequence.
Our cages are self-justifying; we never question
them, and the world is made morally sen-
sible. We win the blame game every time!
We reason backward from consequence
to deed
from effect to cause;
our arithmetic never fails us.
But then sometimes . . . not often . . . but
often enough
Your wonders elude our explanations;
Your miracles violate our confident
calculations,
Once in a while . . .
healing breaks through,
generosity overwhelms our arithmetic, forgiveness moves beyond our
reasoning, hospitality exposes
our careful management.
Beyond our expectation
comes your freighted holiness:
New sight for the blind,
New walking for the lame,
New hearing for the deaf,
New possibility for the poor,
New freedom, new wellbeing,
new joy, All beyond our caged
explanations.

Your holiness breaks our numbness; Your
holiness mocks moral control;
Your holiness opens life beyond our blame
games. We pause in awe before your
transformative power.
We move beyond our management;
We mount up with wings like eagles,
We run in eagerness and are not
tired;
We walk in wellbeing and do
not grow faint.
We are made new well beyond our best
selves. It is no surprise that we break out
in loud praise,
Lost in wonder at your goodness,
Lost in love for the New World you give,
Lost in praise for you . . . you . . . you
alone! Amen.

Walter Brueggemann
March 28, 2022

While Walter's prayers are being compiled today and in various stages of publication, they still have not been integrated fully into his work or seen as the secret window into his exegesis and theological reflections.[2] What Walter invites us to do through his poetry is to wrestle with God. To get down and dirty with God. To interrogate God. To call upon God to be God. To lament with God. To declare God's injustice and deception. To confess our sins. To identify with God's tormented inner self. To lie broken before God. To sing the doxology. To praise. To acknowledge God's otherness. To acknowledge our Creator. To recognize that we are but dust.

Walter's mystical prayers remind us that it is through prayer that we confront the text and the God of the text. Prayer is not separate from the text nor the text from prayer. His prayers are formed as the text informs his prayers. And it is from this exegetical and dialogical prayer life that Walter connects with the living God of the text and from which everything he writes emerges. The prayers reflect the integrated nature of Walter's spirituality, in which prayers out of the text, the study of the text, singing the old hymns of the text, preaching of the text, writing that emerges from the text, social action motivated by the text, and fellowship formed by the text all merge into one. The deed is not separate from the word. Evangelism is not separate from social justice as witness. This approach defies the Enlightenment impulses to differentiate, dissect, and divide the self from itself, from others, and from God. It is a recovery of the ancient ideals which Max Weber saw as the only antidote to a captivated and domesticated people. Walter Brueggemann is not ahead of his time but behind the times. And it is from behind and underneath that the text and the God of the text always comes to reckon with our domestication and acceptance of other gods.

In his prayers, Brueggemann issues a call to modern people who crave certitude, a call back to a poetic world of probing imagination. Back to ancient words that give life, give meaning, and illuminate the wholeness of God in the holiness of God. If we're going to find God, we must seek beyond our modern ways of being. Walter's honest prayers speak to so many people because he gives people permission to bring all of who they are to God. The church has often "silenced" people by suggesting that we can't bring our negative emotions, doubts, and fears to God. Walter's willingness to speak frankly with God and point out that all of this is in the Bible is liberating for many. Of course, not everyone finds his perspective attractive. In one public engagement

at a prominent church, he responded candidly about
God "being in recovery" from the violence that God
had promoted in the Old Testament. In response, the
moderator jumped in and called the service to a close.
Ambiguity about the Almighty just doesn't sell well to a
comfortable people.

Differently Recruited

(On reading Jeremiah 1:4–10)

We live in a society of private self-possession.
    We are summoned every day to maxi-
        mize our freedom,
           to satisfy our hungers and thirsts,
           to find our best path of self-
               actualization,
           to give in to whim or preference or
               inclination.
    We are drawn into such self-awareness,
        because its force is compelling,
        because its promises are attractive to
           us, and
        because its possibilities suit us well.
We could do that: self-possessed, self-
    actualizing, self-aware, self-indulgent . . .
    EXCEPT!
    Except for you,
        and your book and your people!
But we belong to this book, and we say, "The
    Word of God for the people of God."
But we belong to that people, the ones all the
    way back to the Exodus and on to the
    surprise of Easter. They are our folk!
We belong to the book that is filled with
    your old stories that we love to tell.

We belong to this people that has signed on
    in covenant with you.
    In that book and in that people you meet
        us,
        with summons,
        with assurance,
        with obligation, and
        with promise.
You give us work to do,
    work with widows, orphans, immigrants,
        and poor people.
You send us on our way,
        with words to speak,
        with policies to enact,
        with protests to perform, and
        with votes to cast.
You include us in your great work of justice
    as you monitor the rise and fall of
        nations.
You recruit us for your great work of
    compassion,
    as you attend to "the least" among us.
You sign us up for the dangerous work of
    truth-telling,
    as you expose the fakery all around us.
        We are reluctant about your call;
        We are resistant to your summons;
        We are reticent about our mandate;
    But you have said, "Do not fear."
    You have said, "I am with you."
    You still say, "Get moving to where I
        send you."
And we do; we move in obedience beyond
    our self-possession;
    We do it gladly, or fearfully, or partially.

But we do it, because we are your faithful
people.
More than that: You are our faithful God.
So we move, against the current, caught in
the forceful eddy of your purpose. Amen.

It is arguable that before one reads anything else
by Brueggemann, one should begin with his prayers.
In reading his prayers one comes to understand a bit of
his heart, to understand the energy, the source of illu-
mination, the source of the mystery. And that mystery
always emerges from the text. This saturation in the text
is the context out of which *The Prophetic Imagination*
emerged. His capacity to imagine an alternative world
to the one that lies in front of us comes from spending
so much time in a text for which the primary message is
of that alternative world. His was not the view of a scientist or a technician or specialist. It was the view of a poet
who lived within the world of the poets of the biblical
text and who illuminated the way before him.

A Way Illuminated

(On reading Psalm 119:105–12)

Our path of life bears all the marks of our
faith:
That path has its vexations and afflictions
that we readily offer to you;
That path rings loudly with doxologies of
wonder that we voice to you;
That path is filled with snares that seduce
us.
We walk that path of faith as best we can.
But . . .
–sometimes we are cowardly and follow the crowd;

–sometimes we are clever and choose
our own fanciful way;
–sometimes we are forgetful and
imagine we are on our own;
–sometimes in our weariness we just
refuse to move.
But then—in ways that surprise us—
Your good word illumines our path and
shows us the way;
Your good word in scripture offers clear
guidance to us:
In its pages we find evidence of your vast
holiness that undergirds our world;
In its chapters we are given assurances that
sustain us;
In its verses we are given mandates toward
our neighbors;
In its narratives we hear, over and over, your
gifts of life;
In its poems and songs, we are given expansive visions of your good rule.
For the light of your guidance, we are
grateful.
From Moses through Jesus,
we are grateful.
We will walk that path with courage,
not misled,
not deterred,
not delayed or interrupted,
following your lead,
trusting your faithfulness,
abiding in your truth,
all day,
every day,
right to the end. Amen.

One sees the ambivalence and ambiguity in Walter's self about the text and the God of that text. One finds courage and hears the call to courage in the prayers because that's what Walter was always doing. Calling himself to courage as he called others to courage to stand in the face of the empire. Courage to stand in the face of royal consciousness. Courage to stand in the face of God and to tell God to stand up and be God. And one who has the courage to tell God to be God certainly has the courage to tell the empire to be merciful, to show the empire its injustice, to remind the empire of its short-lived power, and to remind the empire that in front of it lies an alternative reality that doesn't have the empire's name on it.

In these Psalms or poems or prayers, one also finds Walter railing against modernity and rationality in a world and a church that has tried to control God. To constrain God. To define God on its own terms. To domesticate God. To make God the god of the empire. Walter is calling us to see the alternative reality of Joshua and Caleb (Numbers 13:1–33). The other ten spies saw giants—they saw grasshoppers. The others saw death. They saw life. At the intersection, they saw freedom, while everyone else saw fear.

A Highway for Holiness

> (On reading Isaiah 40:3–5; see 35:5–7)

A voice breaks our silence;
>   Our silence is a convenience of indifference;
>   Our silence is despair in our impotence;
>   Our silence is a comfort in our self-
>   sufficiency.
And then you speak; you issue
>   imperatives:

    Prepare,
    Make straight,
    Make low,
    Make a plain!
We watch our old landmarks being moved
    in upheaval;
We notice our old certitudes being
    undermined.
We observe our old boundaries being trans-
    gressed.
    The earth trembles before the Earth-
        mover;
    Our world is shaken by the great
        Earth-shaker.
Our world is now labeled "under cons-
    truction,"
    as you build, dismantle, and rebuild,
        making new what was old,
        making vibrant what was tired,
        making possible what seemed too
          hard.
A path is cleared:
    Your holiness enters;
    Your glory marches;
    Your sovereignty advances.
We watch in dazzlement for your presence;
We see you in your glory leading the parade
    of newness,
        followed
    by signs of your great power,
    by the presence of innocent, vulnerable
        lambs,
    by the blind with open eyes;
    by the deaf with ears unstopped;
    by the lamb who dances in delight,

by the speechless who sing new songs,
by the jackals, gators, and lions who
gather to drink.
We have expected you to come alone in your
splendor.
And now we see your great company of
companions,
young, old, great, and small,
a whole realm of new life
in the wake of your holiness.
We gaze in wonder;
We see in disbelief,
and then we sign on,
we join the parade,
we sing and dance and rejoice
because your governance is visible among
us;
We say to each other and to all the others
"Our God reigns,"
And we respond with loud Hallelujahs!
Amen.

One hears throughout these prayers the legacy for which Walter hopes he is most remembered. For his work on the Psalms of lament. Walter brought lament back into the church liturgy. Walter gave permission for the church to accept and acknowledge before God its loss, grief, anger, and will to violence, given the trauma in the world. While so much of evangelicalism is triumphal and exuberant and lives only on Sunday, Walter has brought back Friday. He helped us to understand that we live still on the Friday side of Easter so much of the time. That Easter Sunday did not do away with Friday. That death and dying and grief and pain on Friday are side by side with the praise and doxology that emerges on

Sunday. Lament is antithetical to the nauseating gluttony and entertainment of the empire. Lament in the face of the empire forces the empire to see itself as it is, as cruel, callous, and calculating. Lament in its destitute humanity chips away at the objectified realities and denials of structures of legitimation on which the empire is built.

Welcomed at the Reunion

(On reading Psalm 133)

There was a time . . .
> before Cain killed Abel,
> before Jacob fooled Esau,
> before Absalom killed Adonijah.

There was a time—we can hardly remember it—
> when there was pleasurableness in the human family.

There was such a time in your sovereign hope,
> a time before fear and hate and violence,
> a time before division and hostility and separation.

Such a time it was . . .
> when we had not divided into warring companies;
> when we did not draw harsh lines of
>> race, or nation, or ethnicity, or gender.

Such a time was as your will for creation that you called "good":
> Such a time is like a homecoming of sisters and brothers;
> Such a time is like gifts given all around and sweet foods plentiful for all.

Such a time is for wistful storytelling,
    deep remembering, and passionate
    hoping.
Such a time is like sweet-smelling new-
    mown hay, like a newborn calf that
    can barely stand.
And so, Lord of all our times,
    We pray for such a time of peaceableness
        among us now,
            A time without sword or spear but
                plentiful with plowshares and
                pruning hooks,
            A time of easy travel without menac-
                ing borders,
            A time of compassionate justice,
                and generous infrastructures of
                wellbeing.
We do not doubt your good blessing over
    your world;
        Give us the freedom to trust your
            blessing;
        Give us mercy to share your blessing;
        Give us the energy to perform your
            blessing;
We will all dance and sing and laugh, right
    through the night
    like a family at ease,
        glad for its past,
            eager for its future,
                confident in a present with-
                    out fear or threat.
What a time that was!
What a time that will be!
What a time it is now, in the orbit of your
    blessing. Amen.

Walter's prayers run through with the theme of restoration, which is that alternative reality that lies in front of us; a reality not made of human hands. The alternative reality is always God's reality, the reality of a lion laying down with the lamb and a little child leading. Restoration flies in the face of the newness of the latest commodified thing, in the face of the latest gimmick, bright lights, and shiny toys, which are not new but reiterations of what that which is old. It is only the newness of God's life that is real and true. These prayers run through with the theme of community which is so crucial for the conversation that builds our worlds, a conversation that creates our worlds.

These prayers, as Walter took them into a classroom, were another way of creating a deeper community. Everywhere Walter went he was forming communities, even though he is an introvert; for he understood the importance of being in a community, of creating communities, of contributing to communities where the alternative reality is seen and we can be drawn into it.

Yet Again Raised to New Life

(On reading Psalm 126)

We remember your restorations that have
astonished us:
  We remember healings when life had
  failed;
  We remember communities of loss that
  have rallied in generative ways;
  We remember shame that immobilized
  us,
    and then your shining presence made
    us like new.

We remember old war wounds,
 of cities wrecked, economies laid
  low, and then renewal and
  restoration.
We have the complete inventory of your
 wonders,
 of blind folk who see,
 of lame folk who walk,
 of deaf folk who hear,
 of lepers who are healed,
 of poor folk who have good news of debt
  canceled.
Everyone could see the newness when it
 happened,
 everyone can join the celebration,
  everyone can sing praise to you, great
   restoring God.
And now, now yet again, we wait for your
 newness:
 we witness the brutality of war;
 we fear new versions of a virus;
 we caution about our fragile economy;
 and each of us with a load of worry, anxiety, hurt, or loss.
So now, good God of new life,
 yet again,
  act again in power and goodness,
  act in faithfulness and generosity
   toward us,
   restore us,
   revive us,
   repair us,
That our tears may turn to joy,
That our weeping will become loud
 laughter,

and our sadness will become elated
gratitude.
Do now what you have done before;
Do for us what you have done elsewhere;
Do newness, that we may have life abundant,
you—creator, savior, healer . . .

in our need and our hope, we pray to
you. Amen.

Praise runs through these Psalms and prayers and poems. Brueggemann has made it clear in his work the doxology characteristically comes at the end of lament. For the doxology itself is also a form of resistance to the empire, to the powers and principalities that rule the earth. The praise of God is nothing more and nothing less than an expression of our confidence in God. In the otherness of God. The holiness of God. The aliveness of God. The mercy of God. The justice of God. The mercy of God. The sovereignty of God. Lament and praise create complications for the flattened, deadened world of the empire, an empire that prefers sleeping consumers to praising prophets or poets. That prefers games to those who create their own games and intoxication that covers pain to the honest lament that acknowledges its need for a vision of an alternative reality.

Followers Unburdened and Unencumbered

(On reading Philippians 2:1–11)

We know too much about the church.
We know that the church can be a meeting of petty people
who are preoccupied with such small
stuff,

who readily quibble about triviality,
who spend excessive energy on lesser
things.
It has always been so,
quarrels about syllables,
arguments about dollars,
preferences writ as large as dogma,
mantras repeated too often without
thinking.
It was the work of the great apostle to call his
churches back to their gospel roots.
It continues to be the great work of ministry to remind us:
we are not a political party, or
an ideological pressure group, or
a special interest group seeking our
advantage.
We are—nothing more and nothing less—
than the company of your disciples.
You, Lord Jesus, have said to us, "Follow
me,"
Follow me in courage to places
of need and trouble;
Follow me to venues of power
and coercion,
Follow me in living toward
otherwise.

And we, we may turn from our small agenda
back to the plain truth of Jesus.
We gladly confess you to be "sent from
heaven above."
We willingly acknowledge that you were an
ordinary man who lived your life in vulnerability and risk.

Or as we say, you were filled with God but
emptied your life in humble obedience
to that Other Governance.
We follow you as Lord, not because you are a
noble figure of grandeur,
but rather a man of sorrows and
acquainted with grief.
You always went to trouble spots in order
to do your inscrutable transformative work.
You traveled light and in your enigmatic
authority, you commanded the
demons.
And we . . . in our discipleship . . .
may be like you when we follow,
traveling light,
acquainted with the grief of the world,
always at the trouble spots among
our neighbors,
able to do our own transformative
work, casting out the demons of
death that are among us.
We may imagine ourselves differently as the
church,
unencumbered by demanding property
and habit,
unburdened by quarrels,
undeterred by triviality,
obedient—fully and gladly obedient
to that other sovereignty.
In your obedience, you were raised to honor
in God's presence.
And we, in our glad obedience, may be like
you, be raised into the honor of God's
ultimate mercy. Amen.

Emancipation has been an important movement throughout Brueggemann's life as he's pivoted from moralism to freedom, from conformity to freedom, and from control to freedom. But this has not been a self-seeking navel-gazing journey for Brueggemann. It has been tied directly to his preaching in his teaching and his prayers and his understanding that the text was written for those who need freedom. The text was written for those who hope for freedom. The text was written for those who die imagining deliverance.

Emancipation and deliverance and Exodus are antithetical to the empire's reason for existence. It is antithetical to a church that is domesticated and without energy or courage for its mission. It is no wonder that an enslaved church would embrace the enslavement of Africans coerced to build up the economic foundations of an enslaved empire. The church as much as any social institution engaged in the brutal oppression and dehumanization of enslaved peoples. Church people went to Sunday School and from there took a picnic lunch to a lynching. Many times throughout history the church has been so domesticated by the empire that the lines have blurred between them. Brueggemann continually reminds us that we are separate from the state apparatus, the economic–industrial complex, the military–industrial complex, and the educational–industrial complex. The function of all of this rational modern complex is to pacify and lull the untexted and detexted church into fatigue and denial and sleep.

Throughout Walter's prayers we frequently see the themes of remembering or restoring or putting back together. Exile in Babylon was a time for remembering and writing the Torah. So often it's only in exile that we begin again to piece back together the fragments of our lives and life with God. It's in this space that God can give us a new orientation. Walter's prayers are full of the hope that comes as we look beyond the temporary nature of empires, the temporary nature of our existence, and to the permanence of God.

Fresh from the Word

(On reading Isaiah 55:10–13)

At the outset there was the silence of despair.
And then You spoke:
> You said, "Let there be light."
> You said, "Let my people go."
> You said, "Comfort, comfort my people."

Your word became flesh before our very eyes:
> Light became creation;
> Emancipation became covenant people;
> Comfort became homecoming.
>> Your word is not empty, but full of
>> futures.

You said, "Love God" and we are summoned.
You said, "Love neighbor" and we are implicated.
You said, "Follow me" and we are on a different way with you.
> Your word, in its life-giving power, addresses us every day.
> Your word, in its life-dispatching force, empowers us every day.
> Your word, in its restorative passion, makes new every day.

We are creatures of your word;
> we cannot be otherwise;
> we would not choose to be otherwise.

> It is because of your faithful word that we are
> on our way . . . rejoicing;
>> on our way in freedom,
>> mercy, compassion, and
>> justice,
>> on our way to neighborly
>> wellbeing,
>> on our way rejoicing. Amen.

The prayers of Walter Brueggemann are not tangential to his other work nor are they appendages to be ignored. They are at the secret core from which all of his work and writing emerge. Brueggemann's mystical prayers remind us that true emancipation is only found in our connection to God and the text of that God. And that text and God will always move us to the margins. And in the margins among God's people we will see that all along we were constrained and captivated. And we will begin to care about justice and freedom for the captive, and sight for the blind, and food for the hungry, and clothes for the naked, and water for the thirsty. From that place, we will see most clearly the alternative reality and that it is closer to us than we had ever been able to see in the middle. And we will begin to work for justice as we sojourn as aliens among aliens.

SEVEN

When Prophets Go

*As to "after death," I only go so far as to trust that my
death will not interrupt the good rule of God, and this is
enough for me.*

Walter Brueggemann

It was the early 1970s and the United States was still in
turmoil. The horrors of racism and white supremacy
remained obvious. Violence in the nation's cities was
high. President Nixon had colluded with white South-
erners to crack down on rising crime—with less than
subtle finger-pointing at Black Americans. They dispro-
portionately felt the punitive and tragic effects. Every
historic step forward for Black Americans is always met
with greater efforts to stall or destroy any progress. Most
white Christians stood on the sideline. The Vietnam
War was resulting in the senseless death and disappear-
ance of young American men and women. Protests and
draft-dodging continued. Women increasingly pressed
for equal rights but found little support among many in
the church. Instead, many women were blamed for the
social ills of the day. If only they would stay home where
they belonged and out of the places they didn't belong.

The church was in a conundrum. The old ways of
doing things were breaking down. The gaps between

clergy and member beliefs were growing. Pastors supported many of the shifts in social attitudes—about sexual morality, the teaching of evolution, the loss of prayer in public schools, and the growing gay pride voices—parishioners much less so. The tensions in society were showing up in the pews. Young people were looking for new answers. Some found them in the Jesus Movement. Some found them in the alternative hippie culture of drugs and rock and roll. Some turned toward the invitation of Billy Graham to discover or renew a personal relationship with Christ. Some began to mix social concerns with new ways of reading the Scripture.

In his small, dark hideaway at Eden Seminary, Walter Brueggemann was wrestling with the same concerns as he wrote. He knew that the historical-form criticism of theological studies was partly to blame for the church's crisis. The old mode assumed the biblical text had little to say about the current events, but he had intentionally chosen Union Seminary because it was the only place offering a different approach to the biblical text. His Eden Seminary adviser, Professor Whiston, had steered his student toward Union. He knew that anywhere else would only bore Walter, who already showed signs of being a serious scholar whose priority was serving the church. He was in many ways a reflection of Gerard von Rad, a Confessing Church pastor who would have a significant impact on Brueggemann. Having survived the Third Reich's persecution of the faithful remnant of the church, he was assigned an academic position at Heidelberg where he promoted an interpretive theology that had something to say to the church. Along with maverick James Muilenburg, von Rad deeply formed Brueggemann's exegetical mode. As he wrote in his hideaway, aware of the turmoil in the church and lack of a relevant message from the church to society, Brueggemann wrestled with what the biblical text had to offer.

How did this historic moment reflect 587 BCE? How did the sins of God's people then offer insight into the sins of God's people now? How had the church in a parallel way abandoned those on the margins? How had the church been domesticated by the empire of the day? Signs that the church was joining the empire were everywhere. Even Billy Graham's efforts to get close to every US president smacked of a desire for political influence for evangelicals. Jerry Falwell, a little-known preacher in Virginia, began to put together the skeleton for a social movement that would fully align itself with the Republican Party by the end of the decade and help sweep Ronald Reagan into power. A religious awakening in America was stirring, but an awakening that was more a generic civil religion than a faithful return of God's people to the biblical text for answers. Royal consciousness had always been too great a temptation as compared to "doing justice, loving mercy, and walking humbly with God." The two greatest commandments to love God and neighbor were too ambiguous and open-ended as compared to the evangelical commandments to overturn *Roe v. Wade* and restore prayer in schools and keep gays out of the church. Now those were unambiguous. Justice and mercy and humility had not served Jesus well, so the church would try a different tack while claiming to do what Jesus would do. Everything about the church's approach was antithetical to Brueggemann's upbringing. Love God and neighbor. Be charitable in all things. Pursue ecumenism over religious quarrels. Just how much Brueggemann had internalized his socialization and ancestry was now showing up as he wrote his breakthrough book.

At the same time as Brueggemann was writing, Jim Wallis and other students at Trinity Theological Seminary were looking for a biblical response to the turmoil and injustice they were living in. They responded by forming a magazine, creating an intentional community, and becoming socially active. In 1975, they moved to Washington, DC, and changed their name to Sojourners. Their profile expanded and they discovered a population of like-minded folks who were dissatisfied with the response of the church on both the Left and the Right, progressive and conservative. Though no one remembers how it happened, Brueggemann would write "Better Governance," his first essay in *Sojourners* magazine, in November 1983.

Little did Walter and Jim know that this was the beginning of a forty-year journey in which two individuals from very different paths but with the same passions would find their way together. One was more a theologian and poet and the other more an author/activist, but they spoke the same language, they had the same concerns, and they had the same commitments. They were a great tandem. Walter Brueggemann's writing was just the answer that folks like the Sojourners' crowd was looking for: a prophetic voice who took the biblical text seriously; a theologian whose target audience was the church; a scholar who could write without the need to prove his credentials by using jargon and technical language of the academy; a Christian whose faith commitments saw justice as central to his faith. Over the next forty years, Walter would write forty-three articles for *Sojourners* magazine.

The two had grown up differently. Walter was born in rural Missouri in 1933. A descendant of German immigrants out of the Prussian Union, and Jim was born fifteen years later in Detroit, Michigan. Walter was a member of the Evangelical Synod of North America and Jim of the Plymouth Brethren. Both came from reform traditions shaped by the fatigue of religious quarrels. The Prussian Union formed in 1817 as a forced merger of Calvinists and Lutherans; the Plymouth Brethren originated in 1825 in Dublin, Ireland, reacting to feuds between Methodists, Anglicans, and Baptists. In their reactions, both prioritized the Scripture and simple obedience to it. Both reacted against the organized and institutional nature of the church. The Plymouth Brethren did away with formal ministry altogether, while most Synod pastors had little education and were not highly esteemed. Both grew up with some skepticism of the church. And both had early concerns about racial and social justice. Walter went to the local Black church as a teenager; at fifteen or sixteen, growing up in Detroit, Jim felt like something was very wrong, and nobody was talking about it in his white world. He asked the people around him why white people in Detroit lived such different lives from people in Black Detroit. When he asked questions, the answers were "you're too young to ask these questions," or "we don't know why it's that way," or "if you keep asking these questions, you're going to get into a lot of trouble." So Jim took his questions into the inner city and got work alongside young Black men and in factories. He listened to their stories and went to Black churches, seeking answers from Black church leaders.

The partnership between Wallis and Brueggemann deepened Wallis' theological grounding and provided application of Brueggemann theology to contemporary issues of social justice. And together they amplified the other's prophetic voice.

On June 22, 2018, when Walter was no longer traveling to speak and lecture, Jim asked if he would give a presentation at the annual Summit of Sojourners. Walter agreed. The presentation was entitled "Jesus Acted Out the Alternative to Empire," and, in some ways, Walter ended where he had begun with Sojourners forty years prior—speaking of prophetic imagination. He shared that prophets must be understood as being in a context of totalism. Totalism is the enemy of imagination. It seeks total control, threatens any possible allies of the prophet, and creates economies where the gains go in one direction only. Totalism arms itself at the cost of the marginalized and seeks to control all technologies. It eliminates alternative views of the socially constructed reality of the totalists. Thus prophets are usually detained or destroyed. And then, as if reflecting on his essay from 1983, he shared that prophets understand the "governance of God." They appear out of nowhere. With no credentials. And they say that "God says." They are always poets. They believe God is a lively character who is a real agent in the world. And the task of the prophet is to identify the totalism, reveal the contradictions that sustain totalism, and offer an alternative reality to that of the totalism that lies in front of us. But,

> The practice of prophetic imagination, as you know requires energy, courage, freedom, and the sense of being otherwise. And I have no doubt that we are arriving at a moment where there is no more middle ground. That we either sign on uncritically to the totalism, or we take on this task of dangerous oddness that exposes the contradictions and performs the alternatives.[1]

Walter concluded by appealing to the institutional church to deepen its engagement in Scripture while doing keen and attentive social analysis.

Finally, I want to make a comment—and then I'll be finished—about the institutional church. The institutional church is a very weak instrument for the prophetic imagination. But it is the best instrument we've got. It is the best instrument we got because when people come to church they expect us to talk funny. They expect us to talk about God. And I believe we are now at a point when the church has got to recover its nerve and its energy and its courage and its freedom. To be about our proper business, the church cannot engage in prophetic imagination as long as it lives in the cocoon of totalism. And that of course is where many clergy and laity want the church to stay. Because you get rewards for that, and you get money, and you get payoffs, and you get success. But our mandate and vocation is otherwise.[2]

At the same time, God as an agent is present and at work through the spirit of Jesus who, above all, acted out an alternative.

When he was done speaking at the Sojourners summit the whole audience gave Walter a standing ovation—something they said they had never seen in response to a video presentation. Jim Wallis's response: "This is really a Bonhoeffer moment. Hitler depended on the German Church to rise to power, and only the German Church could have stopped that rise. I can't think of anyone better at theologizing, and everything Walter has written is a theology against white nationalism."[3]

The similarities between the two are striking. Again, one is a theologian, one a practitioner, but both are committed to the same God in the same text. Walter finds himself disappointed with those on the Left, with progressives who have abandoned the text. He is disappointed with those on the Right who have captivated and captured and domesticated the text. Walter has carved his way through by hanging on to the biblical text as the foundation for everything he says, teaches, and preaches. Jim Wallace himself says, "Don't turn left and don't turn right. Go deeper. Don't go right. Don't go left go deeper. Go deeper into the text." Most prophets have sidekicks. Moses had Joshua, Elijah had Elisha, and Jeremiah had Baruch. Mary had Elizabeth. In this case, it's hard to tell who the sidekick is—Jim or Walter. Or perhaps they've both served that role for the other.

Either way, over the last forty years, this powerful duo has moved the church forward. They understood that social justice is not a progressive thing or a conservative thing. It's not a blue thing or a red thing. It's a Christian thing. It's a biblical thing. It's the gospel thing. It's the Jesus thing. The relationship between Jim Wallace and Walter Brueggemann gives some insight into what happens when prophets leave us. We begin to see them as vessels who were usurped by their burning bones, given courage not their own, who walk into danger knowing they have no choice. But in their faithfulness, they leave behind the text and leave behind the words we needed, and still need, to hear. Words that imagine an alternative to the world that lies in front of us. We begin to see that they always knew they were less impressive than the words they offered.

Moses was saved as an infant for the sake of that call that lay ahead. Getting ahead of YHWH, he avenged the death of an Israelite. Escaping to the desert, YHWH met with him in the fire. That fire ignited stumbling lips. Those lips uttered an alternative reality for God's enslaved people. Again and again, he was faithful.

Again and again, they resisted. He finally threw a tantrum that they—and maybe God—deserved. For all he did and said, YHWH prevented Moses from passing into the Promised Land. Led to the top of a mountain, God showed him that the alternative reality was indeed real. Then YHWH led him to his grave. The prophet was gone. But God's words remained. God remained.

Balak, the king of the Moabites, ordered Balaam to curse the Israelites. Balaam panicked when he realized that the prophetic word he received was a blessing and not a curse. He fled on his donkey until it spoke to him and he spoke back. The donkey warned him of the angel with a sword who stood in their way. Balaam returned and blessed God's people seven times, despite the fury of his king, Balak. Balaam whined that he could only speak the words that YHWH gave him, but then he conspired with Balak to lead God's people into sexual sins and idolatry; a scoundrel of a prophet. Regardless of his evil intent and the evil within him, he was the vessel who pointed to an alternative reality even against his will. Regardless of the character of the prophet, the words of YHWH will be spoken. Sometimes even through an ass!

YHWH knew Jeremiah before his conception. YHWH called him as a child. Jeremiah protested that speech was not his thing. YHWH put words in his mouth, and made him an iron pillar, a bronze wall, and a fortified city. Jeremiah did all that YHWH asked, spoke all that YHWH said to him, pointed to the alternative reality of Babylon coming from the north, and then of the ultimate return from their exile. Baruch the scribe wrote it all down—twice. Jeremiah warned God's people against going south and back again to Egypt, and they promised to do what he said. In the end, they did what they wanted, including taking Jeremiah with them. They couldn't live with this recalcitrant prophet, and they couldn't live without him. In Egypt, he railed against their worship of foreign gods. They didn't care. Tradition suggests they finally stoned him to death. The prophet was gone, but God's words remained living and free and open. So did the text. So did YHWH.

Mary was just a child, an ordinary peasant girl. Until an angel called her by name and told her who she really was: a prophetess who would bear God. She accepted the call, more quickly than the men who came before. She didn't protest. She didn't resist. Then she spoke of an alternative reality to the oppression and empire that exploited God's people now. The proud scattered and the powerful dethroned and the wealthy emptied. The lowly lifted and the hungry filled and the words of the prophets before her fulfilled. In the end, she accompanied God to the cross—to God's death. That is the last we hear of her. The prophetess and mother of God was gone. But the alternative reality she spoke of was closer now. So was the Word she brought into the world. So was God.

What happens when prophets leave the world? What becomes of their words? Moses, Jeremiah, Balaam, and Mary remind us that divinity can move through just about anybody. The words of God depend not upon the vessel, The text always trumps the character of the trumpeter. If not, we would have very little text. The Scripture shows no affinity for cancel culture. Many of the heroes of Hebrews 11 would be canceled by Left and Right in today's climate. The legacy the prophet leaves behind lies less in who they were than in the alternative reality that they shared. Their legacy is that they spoke the words they had no choice but to speak, given to them by a God who trapped them until they did so. All prophets remind us that they too

are cracked pots through whose crackedness the light of
that alternative reality shines. An alternative reality that
every prophet has uttered since Eden: God's justice will
straighten all things out in the end. God will have the
last word. Oppressors will be destroyed. The first will be
the last and the last the first. The middle will move to
the margins and the marginalized to the middle.

They are just cracked clay pots reminding God's
people and the empire that it is the just who live by
faith. That faith is believing an alternative reality to the
one that most days lies in front of us. But that message
is so soon forgotten, and so the prophets arise to help
us remember. To speak words that reconstruct the reality of God's world. To speak words that build worlds
and keep the conversation of divine world-building
alive. But in the end, all prophets go away. Some are
more ready to leave than others. And some we are more
ready to see go than others. But all of them go away, and
God's people are left with the reminder that the prophet
was just God's spokesperson pointing to an alternative
reality. They were obedient because they had so little
choice—be burned in their bones by God's words or be
cornered by a deceptive YHWH.

In the end, they may still wonder if it was all worth
it—did they do anything of value? Their origins from
the margins still give them much to be humble about.
While they faithfully spoke God's words, they didn't
always live that way. The fidelity of God was not always
theirs. The promises God kept, they did not always
keep. The perfection of YHWH was matched by their
imperfection. In a moment of reflection about his own
exiting to eternity, Walter once said:

> I believe, with my whole heart, that there is
> nothing worthy in me of living on or being

resurrected. So for all of those folks who are holding out for a physical resurrection and are in the spot of feeling worthy of that, I want to be clear, I do not feel there is any part of me that is worthy of being rescued, and resurrected. Upon my death, I also have no doubt that whatever there is of me will be fully held and kept safe by God. I believe the gospel.[4]

"We die as we lived," we are told. If that is the case, prophets die with God's word as their final words. They never come to peace with the people to whom they are called. Their words are never fulfilled in their lifetimes. The alternative reality of YHWH that they proclaimed, they do not live to see. But they don't stop. Their bones burn to the end. And they know how unworthy they were to be carriers of those words. But they also know that they too are recipients of the same mercy and judgment of God that they proclaimed over friend and foe alike.

When Walter turned eighty-nine in March 2022, he acknowledged that he thinks of his ending. He is content to leave that ending in God's hands, and again imagines the end of life through the text:

Mostly I think of "fullness of days," a phrase used to characterize Job's ending (Job 42:17). This phrase does not specify age or longevity, but refers to the quality or content of one's life. . . . I have been remarkably blessed, and I have so much for which to give great thanks. . . . But then, in an instant of sober honesty and realism, we may come to see, from time to time, how flimsy and unimportant are our

measurements. We may notice that our arithmetic amounts to very little of significance in
the face of our long-term life with God. Such
sober reality tends to come upon us in our
moments of vulnerability and helplessness
when we notice that our "big numbers" of
productivity, wealth, intelligence, or power
are of no use to us. We might even withdraw from the rat race of measurement for
an alternative life. When we withdraw from
the rat race we may stop our intense passion
for our big numbers . . . . But when we stop
these eager calculations, we may fall, as the
prophet intends, into the practice of steadfast love, justice, and righteousness. But of
course, our usual arithmetic does not work
in these categories. We have to take up a different set of calculations. This may be exactly
what Jesus had in mind when he listed the
elements for entry into a different future:

"I was hungry and you gave me food, I
was thirsty and you gave me something to
drink, I was a stranger and you welcomed
me, I was naked and you gave me clothing,
I was sick and you took care of me, I was
in prison and you visited me." (Matthew
25:35–36)

Thus as I pursue my ninetieth year, on my
best days I imagine that my longevity is of
little import. Much more crucial is the "fullness of days." The Torah, and Jesus after the
Torah, has in mind exactly "full of days" of
neighborly covenantalism. It turns out that
the God who is "our hope for years to come"
is not a scorekeeper, but a neighborhood

administrator who is quite uninterested in our best measurements.[5]

The origins of this book lay in locating a prophetic path for the church in these critical days when so much is at stake, so much at the tipping point, and so much need for an alternative reality, where the church's conundrum today reflects its failure to respond faithfully fifty years ago. The attack on the US Capitol, with Christians singing worship songs and flags about Jesus waving overhead, showed just how much closer we are to history's repeat of Germany and its domesticated church in the 1930s. If things continue down the current path, a remnant reflecting the Confessing Church must emerge. And if it does so, Walter Brueggemann will undoubtedly be seen as a voice of prophetic imagination continuing to cast an alternative reality. And Jim Wallis and Sojourners will be companions walking with us on that journey.

The hope at the outset of this book was to find comfort, to find assurance from Brueggemann that a faithful prophetic path is possible, and perhaps less dangerous than it sometimes seems. But nothing about Brueggemann's story brings such assurance, and nothing about the current condition of the world and the church can bring such comfort. Perhaps the best that this story of one prophet's life can do is give us courage by leading us back to the biblical text, to remind us that when we proclaim the alternative reality to the empire, we are not the first to do so. When we challenge an apathetic church and get kicked to the curb, we are in good company with the heroes of Hebrews 11. When we cry out to God from the depths of our basements, God sees and brings a Walter Brueggemann into our lives. Or a Jim Wallis. Or Mary, Jeremiah, Esther, Moses, and so many others who saw an alternative reality and started down the path that seemed to lead there. Always by faith. And often alone.

Indeed, the church in the United States is in a Bonhoeffer moment and she is weaker than she knows. More domesticated than she is aware and more coopted by the empire than she understands. Never more vulnerable and never more in need of a prophetic imagination than now. Prophets like Walter Brueggemann will leave us. From the cloud of witnesses they will cheer us on, "It's true! The alternative reality we imagined is ahead of you! You only must overcome the powers!"

A Timeline in the Life of Walter Brueggemann

March 11, 1933	Born in Tilden, Nebraska, where his father, August, was a pastor
1935	Moved to Hudson, Kansas, the hometown of Walter's mother
1941	Relocated to Salem, Missouri
1942	Moved to Pilot Grove, Missouri
1944	Relocated to Blackburn, Missouri
1951	Graduated from high school
1951–55	Attended and graduated from Elmhurst College
1955–58	Student at Eden Theological Seminary
June 29, 1958	Ordained by his father, along with brother Ed
1958–61	Attended and graduated from Union Theological Seminary
1960	Married Mary Bonner Miller
1961–86	On the faculty at Eden Theological Seminary
1968	Publication of first book, *Tradition for Crisis*
1969–83	Academic dean at Eden Theological Seminary
1977	*The Land* is published
1978	*The Prophetic Imagination* is released
1986–2003	Professor at Columbia Theological Seminary

1990	President of the Society of Biblical Literature
2003–8	Retired, but continued to work on campus and teach part time
2005	Divorced from Mary Miller Brueggemann
2008–18	Resided in Cincinnati, Ohio; continued to write and lecture
2011	Married Tia Ann Foley
2018	Moved to Traverse City, Michigan; tapered off travel and lecturing, but continued to write

Notes

Preface

1   This was the third major study of Anabaptist groups in the United States, with the previous ones occurring in 1972 and 1989. I gave oversight to the study of Mennonite Church USA as part of the larger project entitled the "Church Member Profile 2006," which also included the Church of the Brethren and the Brethren in Christ. The tensions the study revealed within the denomination would result in major losses in mid-level judicatories, congregations, and members in the coming decades. It was out of this research that I began to ask the question: "What if God's Spirit is dismantling the church because of our failure in God's mission to the world that 'God so loved' (John 3:16) and so loves still? And if this is the case, how do we work with God's Spirit rather than against God's Spirit?" Brueggemann's message in *The Prophetic Imagination* (Minneapolis: Fortress Press, 1978) of God's willingness to take God's people into exile in 587 BCE clearly informed my thesis. This thesis would erupt for me again in May 2020 amid COVID-19, in the development of a podcast (www.centerforpropheticimagination.org) and series of four books entitled *A Church Dismantled—A Kingdom Restored* (Morgantown, PA: Masthoff Press, 2021).

2   Brueggemann, *The Prophetic Imagination.*

3   As a sociologist it did not take long to recognize that Brueggemann saw the world through a sociological lens and tightly connected a prophetic capacity to the willingness and ability of the prophet to see the world as a social analyst. To step back from one's lived and micro-level experience and to understand as objectively as possible how the world works. The capacity to see the micro-level realities from a macro-level perspective is called the sociological imagination by C. Wright Mills; *The Sociological Imagination* (Oxford: Oxford University Press, 1959). Another

way of saying this that Mills uses is that public issues affect or create personal problems. Indeed, God has a way of creating personal problems for God's people when they have lost their way Home. The sociological imagination is not unrelated to the prophetic imagination that requires one to step back from one's own reality to see the alternative that lies in front of us. This alternative can only be seen as we embrace a prophetic or God-given view of the world, the One whose ways are higher than our ways (Isaiah 55:8–9). Brueggemann was not only trained as a sociologist as an undergraduate at Elmhurst College but also continued to read widely in the sociological literature over the course of his career. Doing so in part accounts for the ongoing social relevancy of his theology.

4   In an interview Brueggemann once mused, "Why would anyone want to be a church bureaucrat given the mess the church is in?" Over the course of his career he put relatively little energy into the systems and structures of denominations. This was not true of his seminary experiences, where he willingly served as Dean of Eden Seminary and on curriculum committees as called upon. His understanding of the rationality of the modern world, as predicted by sociologist Max Weber in *The Protestant Ethic and the Spirit of Capitalism* (Germany, 1905), leaves him with little patience with denominational systems and structures that have ways of dismissing mystery, mysticism, as well as prophets and their messages. I have said for years, as one who has consulted with numerous mid-level judicatories and denominations, that there is very little they do that has much impact on local congregations. Most exist to provide employment and have very little capacity to turn their ships around. If they could they would have done so by now.

5   W. E. B. Du Bois, *The Souls of Black Folk: Essays and Sketches* (Chicago: A. G. McClurg, 1903).

6   My 2006 research of Mennonites had showed a chasm within the church that reflected the cultural divide in society in educational levels, rural versus urban residence, regional differences, political differences, and on and on. COVID-19 revealed these differences in startling ways in many congregations that took pastors by surprise. Social media was a megaphone for these differences and added to the divisiveness.

7   It soon became clear to me, as I interviewed those who knew Walter well, that the question of what made him "Walter" was

hard for individuals to answer. This became the guiding purpose of the book, believing that answering this question could reveal the key for a church in crisis, for a church that needed an alternative reality than the one that lay in front of it, and that needed God's word of comfort and courage to move toward and into that reality.

8 I assured Walter from the beginning that he would review and affirm whatever was written. He has read, reviewed, and offered editorial feedback and is aware of all the book contains. At the same time, he has given me wide latitude in the organizing and writing of the book, continually reiterating that "this must be your book, Conrad." He has been characteristically generous and kind and supportive, eagerly engaging in the process from beginning to end. I can't imagine a more gracious and supportive subject about whom to write.

9 From the beginning the goal was to get into the spiritual and sociological basement of Walter's life, and to focus as no one has before on the first twenty years of Walter's biography. In the back of my mind was Peter L. Berger and Robert L. Luckmann's framework of the social construction of reality that insists we are dropped into a constructed world; *The Social Construction of Reality* (New York: Anchor Books, 1966). We learn through objectivation the coordinates of that world, and we internalize that world. The central question or social riddle for me became "What was the constructed world of Walter Brueggemann and what did he accept and reject of that world that shaped who he has become?" Theological ideas don't just appear in our brains, they emerge as they connect with ideas from our early formation. In this way I attempt to "read" Walter's life as he read the biblical text, to do a kind of exegesis of the man in making biographical and historical connections that help to explain his expansive theological perspective. In this way, the book is part biography, part theology, part history, and part sociology—all woven together in an attempt to create a cohesive and integrated script that is true to the man.

10 I found in interviewing Walter that utilizing the theological typologies he had created for the biblical text back upon his life as text created a more open space of reflection. I would soon learn that Walter is so immersed in the text that there is little he writes or speaks where the text is absent. To know Walter is to come to know the biblical text and there is little chance of knowing him without reckoning with his appreciation for the text. As his son

John told me in an interview: "If you tell my dad that God doesn't exist, he has little time for such a conversation." Despite all the theological openness of Walter Brueggemann, he has no openness for the idea that God is not present in the world or that God does not intervene in that world.

11   In conducting research for this book, I read many interviews with Walter. A consistent fact was that the interviewers tended to do more talking than he did. He often responded with "That's about right" or "that's right." I was determined from the beginning that this would be a book about Walter Brueggemann and as close to the voice and character of the man as possible. My role would be that of scribe and interpreter. I trust I have achieved that to a helpful degree.

12   This book might best be called a biographical theology or a theological biography or perhaps a "theography."

13   Samuel Balentine, "'Kingdom Scribes,' For Walter Brueggemann," Society of Biblical Literature, November 2013.

14   Carey helped me cull this book from thirty-two to seven chapters and consistently coached me to have confidence in my own voice. It didn't take me long to recognize that this was an individual who excelled at his craft!

Chapter 1

1   This was one of several characteristics bestowed upon Walter by Old Testament theologian Brevard Childs of Yale. Though the two only met once, Childs disdained Brueggemann's work despite the fact that Brueggemann learned much from what Childs offered in his highly regarded *Introduction to the Old Testament as Scripture* (Philadelphia: Fortress Press, 1979). Childs disdained the openness of Brueggemann's theology and more progressive stance on social issues. Brueggemann regarded Childs work with high esteem and was always troubled by the verbal assaults of Childs on his work. Brueggemann did see Childs as being too confined and less expansive in his perspective of the biblical text than was Brueggemann.

2   Walter Brueggemann, *Tradition for Crisis: A Study of Hosea* (Philadelphia: John Knox, 1968); *What Are Christians For? An Inquiry into Obedience and Dissent* (Moraine, OH: Pflaum Press, 1971); *In Man We Trust: The Neglected Side of Biblical Faith* (Philadelphia: John Knox Press, 1972); *The Vitality of Old Testament Traditions: A Study of Hosea* (with Hans Walter Wolff; Philadelphia:

John Knox Press, 1975); *The Land: Place as Gift, Promise, and Challenge in Biblical Faith* (Philadelphia: Fortress Press, 1977).

3   This is the phrase he has used for decades to describe those whose work ethic he appreciates.

4   The Niebuhr brothers influenced Eden Seminary for several decades, as they moved the seminary toward being a professional graduate school, added social science to the curriculum, and also influenced the movement of the Evangelical Synod of North America into the broader American Protestant mainstream. Brueggemann was shaped by their presence which endured at Eden Seminary for decades after they left. Brueggemann wrote a history of Eden Seminary entitled *Ethos and Ecumenism, An Evangelical Blend: A History of Eden Theological Seminary 1925–1975* (St. Louis, MO: Eden Publishing House, 1975) that describes in depth the formation of the seminary and the strong influence of H. Reinhold and Richard Niebuhr upon the institution and its faith tradition. The current president of Eden Seminary compares Brueggemann's impact on Eden Seminary to that of the Niebuhr brothers.

5   The current president of Eden Seminary, Deborah Krause, credits Walter for having pulled together such a remarkable collegium for such a small seminary.

6   Former students speak in awe of the way that Brueggemann moved across the chalkboard and across the biblical canon at the same time, tying texts together and showing the biblical text to be a coherent and entertaining and dramatic narrative with great relevance for contemporary society. The classroom was a sacred space but at the same time no topic was so sacred that it could not be broached. God was large enough to handle both.

7   The SBL is the oldest and largest professional organization for research and study of biblical literature and the place where an Old Testament scholar must engage in order to be recognized as legitimate.

8   As an adult in later years Walter would head out to see his St. Louis Cardinals play, purchasing "clergy" tickets that the Cardinals sold for one dollar to pastors to encourage them to soften their resistance to Sunday ball games. These were of course seats in the outfield far from home plate.

9   Paul Ricoeur was a French philosopher who taught at the University of Chicago. Though he rejected the idea that he was a theologian, his works crossed into theology. His combination of

hermeneutics and metaphors aligned with and added fuel to the interpretive and rhetorical analysis modes that Brueggemann was honing. Clearly, his mode of exegesis is multifaceted. What makes him such a powerful interpreter of the text is his humility in learning and borrowing from just about anybody. The characteristic ego of many academics was missing from Brueggemann. Just as Brueggemann had internalized the ecumenism of the Evangelical Synod, so he applied that ecumenism to the Academy.

10 José Miranda, *Marx and the Bible*, trans. J. Eagleson (Maryknoll: Orbis, 1974).

11 The attention that Brueggemann paid to twentieth-century developments within sociology cannot be overstated. As the discipline was moving from a structural-functionalist view that critics argued supported the status quo of a capitalist economy and the hierarchy of American society, to a neo-Marxist or conflict perspective, Brueggemann made the same move in his theology and exegesis. He did so because his theology was so committed to application of the contemporary world, because he read voraciously across disciplines, and because he was so committed to a dialogic approach across theological and theoretical perspectives. This nimble approach across his career has allowed him to remain relevant as theories of racism, sex and gender, and other marginalized groups have developed using a conflict perspective in theology and sociology. At the same time, he has continued to utilize a Weberian lens to try to understand the subjective experience of individuals. His capacity to develop creative interpretive tools, apparatuses, and typologies is clearly a reflection of his sociology. It is arguable that, had he not written *The Prophetic Imagination* as a prophetic social analyst, the book would have received little or at least less attention and staying power. While the thesis of a prophetic imagination may be Brueggemann's single sermon, like the biblical text, it keeps speaking to us every time we turn to it.

12 Ricoeur's work was so powerful in part because he combined a phenomenological approach with hermeneutics. In doing so one must involve oneself and one's perspective in the reading and interpretation of a text. In other words, one must bring one's full self to the text or object of study. Walter did so to the biblical text, which made it difficult to separate himself from that text.

13 Karl Martin, "Flannery O'Connor's Prophetic Imagination," *Religion and Literature* 26, no. 3 (autumn 1994): 33–58.

14 Interview with Walter Brueggemann.

Chapter 2

1   For excellent reviews of this history see Hugo Kamphausen, *The Story of the Religious Life in the Evangelical Synod of North America*, trans. John W. Flucke (St. Louis: Eden Publishing House, 1990); Carl E. Schneider, *The German Church on the American Frontier: A Study in the Rise of Religion among the Germans of the West, Based on the History of the Evangelischer Kirchenverein des Westens (Evangelical Church Society of the West), 1840–1866* (St. Louis: Eden Publishing House, 1939); Carl E. Schneider, "The Origin of the German Evangelical Synod of North America," in *Church History* 4, no. 4 (December 1935): 268–81.

2   Émile Durkheim, *Suicide: A Study in Sociology* (New York: The Free Press, 1897/1951).

3   Brueggemann, *The Prophetic Imagination*, preface to 2nd ed., ed. Davis Hankins (Minneapolis: Fortress Press, 2018).

4   Pierre Bourdieu, *The Logic of Practice* (Stanford: Stanford University Press, 1980); Pierre Bourdieu, *Distinction: A Social Critique of the Judgement of Taste* (London: Routledge, 1984).

5   From the Columbia Theological Seminary archives, Walter Brueggemann collection.

6   Max Weber, *Max Weber on Law in Economy and Society* (Cambridge, MA: Harvard University Press, 1954).

7   See Frederick Trost's introduction to the catechism and a recent English translation: *The Evangelical Catechism: A New Translation for the 21st Century* (United Church of Christ Press, 2009). This inspirational little booklet is an effort to remind the church of the importance of "sound" doctrine, a project that Trost and others worked at for many years. It represented an effort to renew the church, but it had little impact and was another sign that the seed of German Evangelical pietism had been thwarted by the merger with the Reformed and Congregationalist traditions. Few remember the deep seed of pietism that was planted by the descendants of the Prussian Union in central Missouri and that remains deeply embedded, though perhaps dormant, in the UCC and just about every white American congregation. The tendency toward the "Americanization" is faced by every religion in the United States. The power of assimilation and movement to a common denominator is strong in the American religious economy. Pietism has difficulty retaining its influence.

8   This motto that emerged from the German pietism tradition was part of the ethos of the Evangelical Synod of North America and

reflected their irenic posture and their reaction to the religious
quarrels of their homeland.

9   Trost, *A New Translation,* 17.
10   Trost, 10.
11   Kamphausen, *The Story of the Religious Life in the Evangelical
     Synod of North,* 12.

Chapter 3

1   Walter Brueggemann, "At the Mercy of Babylon: A Subversive
     Rereading of the Empire," *Journal of Biblical Literature* 110, no. 1
     (Spring 1991): 3–22.
2   James Muilenburg, "Form Criticism and Beyond," *Journal of Bib-
     lical Literature* 88, no. 1 (March 1969): 1–18.
3   Brueggemann, "At the Mercy of Babylon," 12.
4   Elizabeth Schussler Fiorenza, "The Ethics of Biblical Interpreta-
     tion: Decentering Biblical Scholarship," *Journal for Biblical Liter-
     ature* 107 (1988): 3–17.
5   Brueggemann, *Prophetic Imagination,* 21.
6   Dorothy E. Smith, *Institutional Ethnography: A Sociology for
     People* (Lanham, MD: Rowman & Littlefield, 2005). Smith and
     W. E. B. Du Bois share in common a rejection of quantitative
     sociological methods, seeing them as imposing the dominant
     reality's categories upon respondents. They both rejected scien-
     tific, rational approaches to knowing and interpreting reality.
     Both relied much on the stories and words of their subjects.
     Both were more poetic in their research, a reality that the dis-
     cipline did not accept readily. In some ways, their interpretive
     approaches mirrored those of Muilenburg, Heschel, Ricoeur—
     and of course Brueggemann. Marginalized groups are those
     from which the prophetic emerges rather than from the cen-
     ter. Parallel methodological trends were occurring in theology
     and sociology, and Brueggemann was keenly attuned to both.
     While the dominant white, male-led American church was not
     particularly open to theological voices from the margins at the
     time, many were willing to hear Brueggemann's message that
     in many ways reflected marginalized theological voices. Walter
     is the last person to claim that his theological work is original
     and quick to own that he readily gleaned from the writings of
     those on the margins. In doing so he also prepared the way for
     these voices to be more readily heard and valued in the church

and Academy. His focus on emancipation in the biblical text contributed to the emancipation of Black, feminist, and liberation theologies that had been stifled by the dominant American church.

7   Brueggemann, *Prophetic Imagination*, 21.

8   Brueggemann, 21.

9   Davis Hankins, Foreword to *The Prophetic Imagination: 40th Anniversary Edition* (Minneapolis: Fortress Press, 2018). Weber argued that the way out of the iron cage of rationality was a recovery of old ideals and the emergence of charismatic prophets. In other words, to break the rational approach to biblical interpretation it would take going back to the Old Testament prophets and Jesus by a guide who could take us there as well as his recovery of the old biblical ideals of faith and hope.

10   Weber, *The Protestant Ethic and the Spirit of Capitalism*.

11   The Frankfurt School was built upon critical theory that combined Weber and Marx in an effort to address the rise of authoritarianism in Europe. It was critical of the Enlightenment and the rationality it produced, including science, pop culture, and the commodification of just about everything. Critical theorists included Max Horkheimer, Theodor Adorno, and Jürgen Habermas.

12   Walter Brueggemann, *Finally Comes the Poet: Daring Speech for Proclamation* (Minneapolis: Fortress Press, 1989).

13   Walter Brueggemann, *Theology of the Old Testament: Testimony, Dispute, Advocacy* (Minneapolis: Fortress, 1997).

14   Interview with Walter Brueggemann.

15   Walter Brueggemann, *Psalms and the Life of Faith* (Minneapolis: Fortress Press, 1995).

16   Interview with Walter Brueggemann.

17   Walter Brueggemann, *Money and Possessions (Interpretation)* (Philadelphia: Westminster John Knox Press, 2016).

18   Interview with Walter Brueggemann.

19   Walter Brueggemann, *Returning from the Abyss: Pivotal Moments in the Book of Jeremiah* (Louisville, KY: Westminster Fort Knox, 2022).

20   Brueggemann, *Returning from the Abyss*, 150.

21   Wright Mills, *The Sociological Imagination*.

22   Peter Berger, *Invitation to Sociology: A Humanist Perspective* (New York: Anchor Books, 1963).

Chapter 4

1   D. W. Winnicott, *The Child, the Family and the Outside World*, 2nd ed. (New York: Perseus Publishing, 1992).
2   Bradford Winters, "A Conversation with Walter Brueggemann," *Image* 55, https://imagejournal.org/article/conversation-walter-brueggemann/.
3   Interview with Walter Brueggemann.

Chapter 5

1   Terry Fretheim, "Some Reflections on Brueggemann's God," in *God in the Fray: A Tribute to Walter Brueggemann*, ed. Todd Linafelt and Timothy K. Beal (Minneapolis: Fortress Press, 1998), 24–37.
2   Walter Brueggemann, "For Terry Fretheim," Church Anew, November 30, 2020, https://churchanew.org/brueggemann/for-terry-fretheim.
3   William Blake, *The Marriage of Heaven and Hell* (1790–93), quoted in "Introduction," in *God in the Fray: A Tribute to Walter Brueggemann*, ed. Todd Linafelt and Timothy K. Beal (Minneapolis: Fortress Press, 1998), 1.
4   Walter Brueggemann, "Jeremiah: Intense Criticism/Thin Interpretation," *Interpretation: Journal of Bible and Theology* 44, no. 3 (1988): 268–80.
5   The three commentaries were: Robert P. Carroll, *Jeremiah, A Commentary* (Philadelphia: The Westminster Press, l 986); William McKane, *A Critical and Exegetical Commentary on Jeremiah I (Introduction and Commentary on Jeremiah i–xxv)* (Edinburgh: T. & T. Clark, 1986); William L. Holladay, *A Commentary on the Book of the Prophet Jeremiah, Chapters 1–25* (Philadelphia: Fortress Press, 1986).
6   Brueggemann, "Jeremiah," 277.

Chapter 6

1   Much of Walter's working life has been defined by his partnership with Mary Miller Brueggemann, his wife of forty-five years. Walter met Mary as a student at Union Seminary; their life and partnership together continued in their years at Eden Seminary and then at Columbia Seminary. Their partnership was definitional for Walter, as Mary encouraged him in his deep love of the

church and taught him a great deal about generosity. Mary was continually supportive of his work and his many travels. Mary and Walter have been blessed by two sons, James, a cracker-jack wholesale lumber rep, and John, a winsome college teacher, both of whom have brought to their parents joy, pride, and honor. For complex and painful reasons, their marriage ended in divorce in 2005 with regret and a sense of failure on Walter's part. In 2011 Walter married Tia Ann Brueggemann who in his more recent years has been greatly supportive of his work. They have worked together to form a new life that is marked by a love of the church, a passion for theater, their many friends, Tia's generous, thoughtful presence, and of course Walter's continuing, though slowing, work.

2   Those books of prayers already published are *Inscribing the Text: Sermons and Prayers of Walter Brueggemann* (Minneapolis: Fortress Press, 2004); *Awed to Heaven, Rooted in Earth: Prayers of Walter Brueggemann* (Minneapolis: Fortress Press, 2002). Others are forthcoming.

Chapter 7

1   Walter Brueggemann, "Jesus Acted Out the Alternative to Empire," *Sojourners*, June 22, 2018, https://sojo.net/articles/walter-brueggemann-jesus-acted-out-alternative-empire.

2   Brueggemann, "Jesus Acted Out the Alternative to Empire."

3   Interview with Jim Wallis.

4   Interview with Walter Brueggemann.

5   Walter Brueggemann, "Divine Arithmetic," Church Anew, May 11, 2022, https://churchanew.org/brueggemann/divine-arithmetic.

Bibliography

Balentine, Samuel. "'Kingdom Scribes,' for Walter Brueggemann." Society of Biblical Literature, November 2013.

Berger, Peter L. *Invitation to Sociology: A Humanist Perspective.* New York: Anchor Books, 1963.

Berger, Peter L., and Robert L. Luckmann. *The Social Construction of Reality.* New York: Anchor Books, 1966.

Blake, William. *The Marriage of Heaven and Hell* (1790–93).

Bourdieu, Pierre. *Distinction: A Social Critique of the Judgement of Taste.* London: Routledge, 1984.

—— *The Logic of Practice.* Stanford: Stanford University Press, 1980.

Brueggemann, Walter. "At the Mercy of Babylon: A Subversive Rereading of the Empire." *Journal of Biblical Literature* 110 (Spring 1991): 3–22.

—— *Awed to Heaven, Rooted in Earth: Prayers of Walter Brueggemann.* Minneapolis: Fortress Press, 2002.

—— "Divine Arithmetic." Church Anew, May 11, 2022, https://churchanew.org/brueggemann/divine-arithmetic.

—— *Ethos and Ecumenism, An Evangelical Blend: A History of Eden Theological Seminary 1925–1975.* St. Louis, MO: Eden Publishing House, 1975.

—— *Finally Comes the Poet: Daring Speech for Proclamation.* Minneapolis: Fortress Press, 1989.

—— *Inscribing the Text: Sermons and Prayers of Walter Brueggemann.* Minneapolis: Fortress Press, 2004.

—— *An Introduction to the Old Testament: The Canon and Christian Imagination.* Philadelphia: Westminster John Knox Press, 2003.

—— "Jeremiah: Intense Criticism/Thin Interpretation." *Interpretation: Journal of Bible and Theology* 44, no. 3 (1988): 268–80.

—— "Jesus Acted Out the Alternative to Empire." *Sojourners,* June 22, 2018. https://sojo.net/articles/walter-brueggemann-jesus-acted-out-alternative-empire.

—— *The Land: Place as Gift, Promise, and Challenge in Biblical Faith.* Philadelphia: Fortress Press, 1977.

—— *In Man We Trust: The Neglected Side of Biblical Faith.* Philadelphia: John Knox Press, 1972.

—— *Money and Possessions (Interpretation).* Philadelphia: Westminster John Knox Press, 2016.

—— *The Prophetic Imagination.* Minneapolis: Fortress Press, 1978.

—— *Psalms and the Life of Faith.* Minneapolis: Fortress Press, 1995.

—— *Returning from the Abyss: Pivotal Moments in the Book of Jeremiah.* Louisville, KY: Westminster Fort Knox, 2022.

—— *Theology of the Old Testament: Testimony, Dispute, Advocacy.* Minneapolis: Fortress Press, 1997.

—— *Tradition for Crisis: A Study of Hosea.* Philadelphia: John Knox Press, 1968.

—— *The Vitality of Old Testament Traditions: A Study of Hosea,* with Hans Walter Wolff. Philadelphia: John Knox Press, 1975.

—— *What Are Christians For? An Inquiry into Obedience and Dissent.* Moraine, OH: Pflaum Press, 1971.

Carroll, Robert P. *Jeremiah, A Commentary.* Old Testament Library. Philadelphia: The Westminster Press, 1986.

Childs, Brevard. *Introduction to the Old Testament as Scripture.* Philadelphia: Fortress Press, 1979.

Durkheim, Émile. *Suicide: A Study in Sociology.* New York: The Free Press, 1897/1951.

Du Bois, W. E. B. *The Souls of Black Folk: Essays and Sketches.* Chicago: A. G. McClurg, 1903.

Fiorenza, Elizabeth Schussler. "The Ethics of Biblical Interpretation: Decentering Biblical Scholarship." *Journal for Biblical Literature* 107 (1988): 3–17.

Fretheim, Terry. "Some Reflections on Brueggemann's God." In *God in the Fray: A Tribute to Walter Brueggemann,* edited by Todd Linafelt and Timothy K. Beal, 24–37. Minneapolis: Fortress Press, 1998.

Hankins, Davis. Foreword to *The Prophetic Imagination: 40th Anniversary Edition.* Minneapolis: Fortress Press, 2018.

Holladay, William L. *A Commentary on the Book of the Prophet Jeremiah, Chapters 1–25.* Hermeneia. Philadelphia: Fortress Press, 1986.

Kamphausen, Hugo. *The Story of the Religious Life in the Evangelical Synod of North America.* Translated by John W. Flucke. St. Louis: Eden Publishing House, 1990. Originally published as *Geschichte des religiösen Lebens in der Deutschen Evangelischen Synode von Nord-Amerika.* St. Louis: Eden Publishing House, 1925.

Kanagy, Conrad L. *A Church Dismantled—A Kingdom Restored: Why Is God Taking Apart the Church?* Morgantown, PA: Masthof Press, 2021.

—— *Road Signs for the Journey.* Scottdale, PA: Herald Press, 2007.

Martin, Karl. "Flannery O'Connor's Prophetic Imagination." *Religion and Literature* 26 (1994): 33–58.

McKane, William. *A Critical and Exegetical Commentary on Jeremiah I (Introduction and Commentary on Jeremiah i–xxv).* The International Critical Commentary. Edinburgh: T. & T. Clark, 1986.

Mills, C. Wright. *The Sociological Imagination.* Oxford: Oxford University Press, 1959.

Miranda, José. *Marx and the Bible.* Translated by J. Eagleson. Maryknoll: Orbis, 1974.

Muilenburg, James. "Form Criticism and Beyond." *Journal of Biblical Literature* 88 (March 1969): 1–18.

Schneider, Carl E. *The German Church on the American Frontier: A Study in the Rise of Religion among the Germans of the West, Based on the History of the Evangelischer Kirchenverein des Westens (Evangelical Church Society of the West), 1840–1866.* St. Louis: Eden Publishing House, 1939.

—— "The Origin of the German Evangelical Synod of North America." *Church History* 4 (December 1935): 268–81.

Smith, Dorothy E. *Institutional Ethnography: A Sociology for People.* Lanham, MD: Rowman & Littlefield, 2005.

Trost, Frederick. *The Evangelical Catechism: A New Translation for the 21st Century.* Cleveland, OH: Pilgrim Press, 2009.

Weber, Max. *Max Weber on Law in Economy and Society.* Cambridge, MA: Harvard University Press, 1954.

—— *The Protestant Ethic and the Spirit of Capitalism.* Germany, 1905.

Index